REAPING

Inwood
Indiana

Reaping
Inwood Indiana Press
www.InwoodIndiana.com
©2016 Prolific Press Inc.
Editor; Glenn Lyvers
Assistant editor; April Zipser
ISBN: 978-1-63275-071-6
Published by: Prolific Press Inc.
Harborton, VA

Unless explicitly stated, all stories and events depicted in this book are purely the fictional imaginings of the creative author. Any resemblance to actual events or people is purely coincidental and not based in reality. The real people of Inwood are much stranger.

CONTENTS

Felon

One time only
the walls started
to close in. My

head pounded
with sweat damp
beads on my

arms and thighs.
White dirty concrete
pressed against

my burning temples.
No way out.
I was alone

and it was dark
except for the moon
glowing on

the barbed wire
curling over
the fence outside

my window.

~Charles Kell

Too Young to Face the Dawn

Dear Eva,

You are crying now in your crib, which your father moved from our bedroom to the guest room. He sleeps there with you because on your first morning home, when you cried, I cried too and told your father to get you away from me.

It's been two weeks since your birth. I can't speak your name. I say, "It" is hungry. "It" is tired. "It" is wet. I don't want you near my breasts. At least I can write your name, *Eva*. I'll keep writing it. *Eva*. If this is a breakthrough, I'll need to thank my psychologist who prescribed writing you letters.

At your birth, my regular physician was in Barbados. An invader, some pompous resident, checked my dilation with his index and middle fingers. His nails stretched against his glove. "We're still at four centimeters," he said. *We* weren't though. I didn't want him to take the moment from me. That's when I remembered a sardonic memory from my adolescence I had buried —the night I met Pharaoh Kal-Bassari. It spoiled any motherly jubilation, any intimacy I could've felt for you.

In retrospect, since that night, I've sunk like a damaged ship. When that resident touched me, the memory, which rested on the seafloor of my subconscious, bubbled to the surface. I birthed a reminder of the most horrifying moment of my life.

Pharaoh Kal-Bassari molested me. I'm sure of it.

When you're old enough, you will learn of Pharaoh. He's a world-famous surfer. A massive black-and-white photograph of him riding a wave is a permanent exhibit at the MoMA, a few blocks from our apartment in Midtown. I went there. Inscribed below the photo is a quote from Pharaoh, "Humans are made of a multitude of infinitesimal star-seeds." He's a trick, *Eva*. You must be aware of men like him.

My psychologist told me to write to an "adult Eva" who has the ability to judge my actions. I'll begin with my life at sixteen, at my family's Inn, On Borrowed Time. Past where the road ended, our home was at the tip of the outer shore. My mother, Irene, gave directions to guests as follows: "At Exxon station remove 10 psi from tires. Continue until you hit sand. Left at the ocean. In ten miles, turn left between the dunes marked with American flags." Check-in times were dependent on the tides. On Borrowed Time resembled a drip sandcastle. Improbably, the architect had layered rooms on top of steeples on top of cedar closets on top of bay windows to design a structure that somehow withstood blunting storms.

Besides myself, six people were present that night. Mother, who in her youth had served as a Peace Corps nurse, kept one room as free lodging for any marred creature be it clipped egret or stranded sailor. One such weary soul was our only guest that night, John Manatoe. Then, I knew him as the oyster diver who took refuge in the tiniest bed in Mother's care room. The outer shore's far rim ran rough. The crag's base proved fertile ground for pearl oysters.

My father, George, was there—a real penny-pincher; George would've been one of the keepers who told Mary there was no room at his inn. Of course, my molester was there (*Eva, I could bash my head against my desk for using such possessive, but I refuse to erase it*). Also present, his underling, a wretched man, Flipper Sadat, and my friend, Jocelyn.

Jocelyn could be best described in two words, early developer. She claimed her breasts arrived at ten. By fifteen, she'd come to understand their devilry. She arrived as the *au pair* for a vacationing, South African family, the Brummel's, who believed they'd hired an eighteen-year-old. Jocelyn managed to fool them for a month before they left without her. My parents employed her to dress beds, bake waffles, etc.

My education came from the summer guests who carried knowledge from the mainland. Dr. Dahlquist, a zoologist, who spent summers studying bottlenose dolphin migration, would let me hold a preserved brain he carried in his luggage. Jean Arthur, a daffy old widow who claimed to have known Nancy Reagan, chatted with me about politics. I overheard business negotiations by the horseshoe pit and marvelous gossip on the terrace. But in the off-season, we were lucky to book a stray fisherman.

Every day I awoke at blue hour and spent my mornings picking lenticels off tubers for chowder. I lived entire days in my bikini. At night, Jocelyn and I could dial our music to full volume—nothing could be heard over the ocean's roll.

On that terrible night, thunder boomed as the first named storm of autumn, Adolphus, made landfall. A salty zephyr whistled through a crack in my bedroom window. I pushed my forehead against the glass. The sky split. A dark cloud twirled the wispier, eastern ones into its swirl like a fork sucks spaghetti off a plate.

Jocelyn crawled from beneath a gob of worn blankets. She woke the disc player. The opening notes of Juice Newton's "Angel of the Morning." Juice's voice was wispy, with an ache behind each note. Jocelyn and I performed music videos—I played the man who slept with the prostitute, then left her bed before sunrise.

I reached behind me to take hold of the splintered sill. I whipped my hair. When Juice belted the word "dawn" at the end of the second chorus, I somersaulted onto the bed. In sync, we belted the refrain, elongating the words: aaaaaaaaan-gel and baaa-baaa-baaaaaaa-by.

For the dramatic finish, I stepped to the bed's edge and swan-dived into the blankets.

"Why do we even like that song?" Jocelyn asked. Her breathy, South African tinged voice had a certain staccato impulse that characterized a ditzy girl. She sat at the rattan vanity, which was littered with L'Oreal vials. She stretched her eyes and applied liner. She drew in her cheeks and blushed her cheekbones. "I have the oyster diver in a half-hour." She used the blush to powder between her breasts. "Two hundred for the night."

Here, *Eva*, my inclination is to turn to abstract language to hide this simple truth. I've never told your father. I certainly never would've told my child, but my psychologist said to tell my truth. Jocelyn and I prostituted. Her for money, me for trinkets men left.

I received my first gift, an Antarctic penguin egg, when Dr. Dahlquist, wrapped in a towel, put it into my hand and told me he couldn't live without me. I was cleaning the outside showers. He wrung his arm around my midriff and told me Jocelyn had let him touch her breasts. My scrub brush fell and clanked off the bucket lid. Sudsy-water ran beneath my feet and through the thin spaces between the wooden planks.

When I asked Jocelyn, she confessed, yet confession implies guilt—she had none. *Eva*, understand I lived on a cay, tethered to the mainland by an eroding strip. Each year the beach thinned. I prostituted because I wanted Dr. Dahlquist, all the men, to remember me. The girl at the edge of the continent who *did* have something meaningful to offer.

But I never offered Pharaoh anything. He took it.

You've stopped crying. Your father probably picked you up and told you he loves you. I haven't let your father touch me. I can't blame you. You couldn't have known. At your birth, when I remembered that night, shame paralyzed the lower-half of my body, which was propped in stirrups. I didn't want that half of me and worse, I let you enter this world through it.

Maybe my psychologist is right, there can be consolation in that which is most unsettling — so, here, *Eva*, I record the rest of that night unfettered by self-analysis.

"Come with me to the oyster diver's room." Jocelyn pushed her hand through a stack of gold-plated bracelets. "I can charge triple if we go together."
I lit my table lamp, a relic Tiffany with blue dragonfly etchings. Outside, the clouds discharged their electricity, illuminating the sand dunes in purple. In a flash, I saw a man drag another's limp body from the ocean. In another, he had pulled him to the base of our dune. My mother hollered for us.

In our foyer, the littler man, Flipper, tried to pull Pharaoh through the door. He smacked his side into our onyx mirror. It detached from the plaster and fractured into billions of bits across the titled floor.

Pharaoh was leashed to half an electric-blue surfboard. When Mother went to help, Flipper yelled, "Don't touch him."

"He's right," Father said. "Call the Coast Guard." He caught a mirror shard in his slipper and yelped, "Jocelyn, bring a broom."

"Genevieve," Mother called to me. "We need gauze and antiseptic."

We learned later that a wave had split Pharaoh's surfboard. He'd knocked his head against the jetty and his lower-body jammed beneath a rock. Flipper yanked him free, but shredded Pharaoh's legs. He tied Pharaoh's body to the top-half of the board so he could drag him across the beach to our home.

"Let's carry him to a bed." Mother nodded to us.

Flipper panted on the floor. His wetsuit bulged around his pelvis and underneath his armpits. He looked like a piece of soppy bread.

Pharaoh's right calf was torn. The left side of his face rested on the board's nose. He had severe features, synonymous with what we revere as Egyptian beauty: almond eyes, razor-cut cheekbones, an obtruding chin, and a swimmer's torso, hard like a golden sarcophagus. What were indomitable were those nutty eyes, their color reminiscent of a worn encyclopedia.

His eyebrow had been sliced. Blood flowed down his temple, pooled into his earlobes, and ran into his braided hair. Each braid was a rope of starchy fibers. They followed the shape of his head, over the surfboard's lip, and fanned the floor.

5

"Surface wounds," Mother said. She pointed down the hallway to the care room where the oyster diver awaited Jocelyn. We carried Pharaoh to a bed. The A-framed room had six beds. The oyster diver was tucked into the furthest one.

Flipper entered as mother cut off her patient's trunks. Pharaoh looked as if he had already passed. Flipper cried, "Why? Wa-wa-wa-hy?"

"He'll be fine." She cinched an elastic tourniquet above Pharaoh's thigh.

Flipper held his fingertips a centimeter above Pharaoh's abdomen, as if he were not allowed, by rite, to make contact with such a relic. "You're healing Pharaoh Kal-Bassari. He's on a mission to ride godly mountains." Flipper pulled down the top half of his wetsuit. His flabby, welted chest was a stark contrast to the sculpture before me. "Mohammed and the mountain. Mount Olympus. Mount Sinai. The transfiguration." He said it like a question, as if I were dense for not making the seemingly apparent connection. "Every holy man has his mountain."

I always needed proof. *Eva*, I want you to be more like your father, except I hope you will be the type of girl who isn't charmed. Flipper's lofty speech was a lie. If Pharaoh had been blessed, then why did he crash? It seemed simple.

"I guess he'll need to try a smaller mountain," I said.

Flipper grabbed the bed-frame and pointed at Pharaoh's body. "This scar on his collarbone is from a vicious swell in Oahu. The one on his left side, he slipped off a tidal bore in the Polynesian." He got animated, defending Pharaoh's honor. "Surfers have died there." Blotches appeared on his neck and face.

I had punched a nerve. Flipper believed his friend a god. What were we? Servants? Footnoted women, long-forgotten in the legend of Pharaoh Kal-Bassari?

Mother whisked four ointments into a mortar. She dosed Pharaoh's wounds. I heard his skin sizzle, but he remained unmoved.

"He'll live," Mother said with a tinge of mockery.

By the time Mother finished dressing the wounds, Flipper had fallen asleep. Jocelyn too, on the floor. In the far corner, the oyster diver's bare back faced me. The storm had passed, so I thought.

Irene covered Pharaoh's bottom half with a white sheet. She lit a candle. In its light, she kissed my forehead and walked upstairs.

I clicked on a lamp, then shook Jocelyn. She awakened with a jerk and put her hand over her eyes.

I whispered, "The oyster diver's asleep. We should go back to the attic."

"No. Even *bet-tah*." She roused herself awake and removed her tank top. "We'll surprise him." She reached behind me and untied my bikini. Jocelyn, seeming to sense my apprehension—she tweaked my cheeks. "There are much more detestable acts than giving a man some comfort."

Her logic could've justified every despicable human action. Even molestation. If we weigh the morality of our actions against the whole of human wickedness, then our actions will always seem minor. It suddenly felt wrong, but I didn't want Jocelyn to go it alone. We were just girls, too young to face the dawn.

A bamboo coffee table divided Pharaoh's and Flipper's beds from the oyster diver's. Jocelyn smacked her shin right into it. As I reached for her, a hand grasped my thigh. It bound me to my spot on the floor.

The hand pulled me to the bed. I tried not to flinch. "Floating beyond the surf, I put my fingers into the ocean." The hand moved between my legs. "I felt the radiance of every planet and comet charging the water." Pharaoh's voice was as coriaceous as I expected. He pressed his penis against my back. His other hand gripped my stomach. "I saw your window, glowing as proof that I would not drown tonight."

His thumb ran underneath my bikini bottom's elastic band. "You kept me alive."

He wanted to leech something out of me. My childhood or spirit, I still don't quite know. A dreadlock fell onto my bare shoulder. It was scratchy, and I thought it might coil around my neck and strangle me.

I yelled for Jocelyn who hovered above the oyster diver. She hit the floor. Before I knew what had happened, the oyster diver, as massive a man as Pharaoh, stood over us. He dropped his elbow into Pharaoh's peaked chin. Blood laved over his mouth. The diver clenched his fists together above his head and slammed both down into Pharaoh's bandaged upper thigh. Pharaoh howled, but tightened his vise.

Irene entered and turned on the overhead lights.

At this point, Flipper awoke. He stumbled into the backlash of the diver's next blow.

"Stop. Stop." George stormed in. He seized the diver's arm, then, seeing me on the bed, with his other, he smacked me across my left cheek.

The diver grabbed Pharaoh's hair and pulled him to the floor.

I leapt off the bed, but Flipper knocked me down en route to protect Pharaoh from the diver's assault. Jocelyn found me. I couldn't contain my sobs or my embarrassment of being half-naked in front of mother and father.

Pharaoh tried to stand. His legs gave out as they tried to bear weight. He spat blood onto the hardwood, then leaned on Flipper.

After they left, my father looked fixedly on my face. I placed my hands over my breasts. He did not speak. Jocelyn, believing in the morning she'd be tossed out with the coffee grinds, went to the attic to pack. The oyster diver went back to sleep.

My mother always knew things unknowable. Things I'd so thoroughly conceal, even from myself. She wrapped me in a quilt. "Oh, Gen," she said in a voice so full of pity. "It's going to be so difficult." Then, slowly, she turned away.

Here, *Eva*, is another unknowable—will you ever have the great capacity to empathize? No child should be asked to do so. You may forever remind me of that night, or, now fully dredged, maybe not. I so want to love you as my little girl.

In Juice's song, the prostitute asks the man to touch her cheek before he leaves. That's all—a miniscule motion to recognize that their act contained a smidge of love.

The next morning, I approached the diver while he washed a bucket of oysters with our hose. The sun shone strongest the day after a hurricane. I thanked him.

"Do you know how pearls are formed?" He put an oyster into my hand. "It's out of defense, when a foreign substance slips through the oyster's mantle—it coats the irritant with layers of a certain mineral."

I'm not positive of my final motion after Pharaoh left, but I'd like to remember, for our sake, *Eva*, that I took in a full breath—held it in my lungs—held it as if it were a treasure, the beginnings of a pearl.

~Andrew DiPrinzio

Glossoplegia

Randall looked up at the grid pattern of panels in the room's drop ceiling and imagined a board game. The squares of florescent lights would mean something special. The supply and return air ducts would mean something else. Landing on a panel with a sprinkler valve would heal your damage and make you pure. The smoke detector, because there was only one, would award you special powers. The ones with brown water stains must be avoided.

From time to time, a man in a blue jumpsuit would ascend a noisy metal ladder and replace any blotched panels. But he would never fix the leak. They weren't in the business of solving things here. Only treating.

Randall knew the floor had a similar pattern. When they rolled him over, he could see large white tiles stretching to the walls. Between each square was a thin line of grout turned various shades from age and wear. The tiles were manufactured to be identical and the only differentiation came from a few cracks and stains that couldn't come clean.

In these tiles, Randall could not formulate a game. He spent most of his time looking at the ceiling and so little of it examining the floor. Still, he used those episodes to memorize the location of each imperfection. Three tiles down, two tiles to the right on his left side had a hairline crack in the shape of a Y. Against the wall on his right side, four tiles from his bed, rust remained in a set of overlapping circles. He wasn't sure what he would do with this information, especially since it could never be complete. He didn't even know was beneath his own bed. But it was something to do with some of the only parts of him that still functioned.

Other days, Randall imagined the ceiling's main runners and cross tees were streets in a perfect city. Cars would cruise slowly. Pedestrians strolled without a care. A stoplight hung at every intersection. He planned out his metropolis block by block. City hall here, police station there. Fire house, library, park, high-rise apartment buildings, department store, schools, university. No hospital, though. In his city, there was no sickness.

Randall tried not to concern himself with the rest of the room. It was always changing, and by now he was older than everything else in it. With the exception of the floor, most of the ceiling and himself, all the contents had been replaced at one point. The walls were the same, but they had been painted different colors. Twice. Anything once his had been removed, including the basketball that sat on his side table, before it deflated. Sometimes, someone would bump it and it rolled off, the bouncing unbearable.

He measured time by the faces. After he awoke, he would usually see one face four times at regular intervals. Then, he would see another three times, and on the last rotation of Randall's personal clock, the hands belonging to that face would inject sleep. The faces changed over the years, and when they were new, they often spoke. He enjoyed hearing the fresh voices, but they usually fell silent after a while.

Right after the crash, he saw a lot more people. Doctors, specialists, Father McMillan, the guys. Peggy. Coach. Now, only his sister Agnes stops by about once a month, sits at his side and prays a mumbling rosary. His mother used to visit every day. Then once a week. Then not at all, and his sister never said why. His dad was allowed to come, once, to apologize, but his mother stormed in and pounded her fists against her husband's chest before he got a chance to get all the words out.

Randall hoped his eyes, in that moment before they led his father out of the room in handcuffs, had told him he was forgiven. He couldn't bear the thought of his father, bound in his own room, staring up at some unconceivable ceiling, thinking that his son hated him. The family of the others undoubtedly did, but Randall wanted to take on some of that weight. He should have said something that night, should have offered to drive, but he was so exhausted after practice he just rested his head against the cool, foggy passenger-side window and tried to ignore the faint familiar smell—the last scent he'd ever know—emanating from the brown paper bag resting on the seat between his father's legs.

When Randall plays his board game, he never lets himself win. And he doesn't live in his perfect city. But right before his sedative is administered each night, he can't help but use the ceiling like graph paper to pencil in midcourt, three-point and free-throw lines and fade away upon a memory of jumping.

~Bill Lisbon

Eddie Says Goodnight

Nobody in Inwood Indiana talks about Eddie Slabaugh anymore. Why would they, there's nobody left who remembers Eddie Slabaugh.

Sure, he has the same name as the family who run the restaurant in town, but he came from a different branch of the Slabaugh family, distant cousins who lived out on Lincoln Highway toward Bourbon. Eddie was an only child, and when he left for the war in Europe in late 1942 (that's World War Two, the one against Hitler and the Nazis, not one of the many other wars-to-end-all-wars we've had since then), his mother was already a widow.

Eddie was a fly boy, a pilot with the United States Eighth Air Force 100th Heavy Bombardment Group, taking B-17 Flying Fortress planes on bombing raids across Nazi Germany and Occupied Europe. But, Eddie never came back from Europe. His plane was shot down during a raid – the infamous Münster raid in October 1943 – and ditched in the North Sea. There were no survivors from the crew of 10 airmen. No wreckage. No bodies.

And no memorial either! By the time the United States got around to commemorating its dead after the war was over, Eddie's mother had long since died of a broken heart, and somehow poor Eddie Slabaugh fell through the loop. The Air Force forgot about him, and so his name never made it onto any war memorial, not even the one in the old Salem Cemetery at Inwood. Perhaps that's why his ghost still walks the Earth.

But, I'm getting ahead of myself. Besides, we really shouldn't beat up the military for overlooking Eddie. US Eighth Air Force alone suffered 26,000 casualties in World War II, with a further 29,500 flight crew shot down, becoming of prisoners of war who then had to be extricated from the ruins of Nazi Germany and repatriated.

For those of you unfamiliar with 100th Heavy Bombardment Group, you might have heard their unfortunate nickname of the "Bloody Hundredth." They earned it for the higher-than-average number of casualties they sustained. On some raids, over a dozen planes would be lost and in the case of the Münster mission just one plane – Rosie's Riveters – returned safely to its base in the East of England. (That's as in England, UK not New England, USA.)

In all, during the course of the war, the Bloody Hundredth lost 177 planes in the course of flying 306 missions. If you can find a copy on DVD, you might check out the 1949 Oscar-winning movie "Twelve O'clock High," which stars Gregory Peck and is based on the missions flown by the 100th and other groups within the US Eighth Air Force.

Military historians suggest two possible explanations for the Bloody Hundredth's high attrition rate. The first is poor leadership and discipline, resulting in planes not flying in sufficiently tight defensive formations, so enemy fighters could penetrate the "killing zone" and pick off planes. Eddie Slabaugh, incidentally, was one of the pilots reported for frequently flying out of formation.

The second is the so-called "wheels down incident" in early 1943, one B-17 lowered its wheels in surrender, when it got into difficulties over Germany, but then apparently changed its mind and shot down the escorting German Messerschmitt fighters. This, not surprisingly, made the 100th a "marked outfit" for Luftwaffe pilots.

You've guessed it, Eddie was the pilot of that B-17, although he subsequently claimed it was all a misunderstanding, that he had never signaled his intention to surrender, and anyway it was a mechanical fault that caused the landing-gear to come down mid-flight.

Of course the Bloody Hundredth may just have been dogged by bad luck. Whatever the reason, other American bomber groups liked flying with the 100th "because the Nazis go after them instead of us."

This is where I enter the story because I was researching a history book about the legends and myths of East Anglia when I came across the story of Eddie. East Anglia was (and still is for that matter) a relatively flat, thinly populated agricultural area on that part of the UK that bulges out into the North Sea. In World War II, this made it the perfect location for airfields that were the shortest distance flying-wise from Enemy Europe. In fact, it proved such a popular location that by the end of the war there were over 200,000 US Eighth Air Force personnel stationed there, earning it the nickname of "The Fields of Little America."

But, I digress. The Bloody Hundredth were based at the Thorpe Abbotts airfield, known to the Americans as USAAF Station 139. After the war, the station closed and was turned back over to agricultural use, with most of its buildings, runways, hard-standing, and perimeter track being broken up. However, in 1977, the control tower and several other buildings, including a couple of Quonset Huts, were leased to a group of volunteers who set about restoring them and creating what is now The 100th Bomb Group Memorial Museum.

But, from time to time, visitors to the museum have reported an overpowering "presence" within the control tower.

Sometimes it is accompanied by a brief glimpse of an airman dressed in full flying gear. Sometimes the sound of VHF radio chatter and the noise of aircraft has been heard. Even museum volunteers will admit that, after locking up the control tower at the close of the day and walking to their cars, they have turned back to see an airman standing at a first-floor window, looking out as if to say good night. And then there is the whistling, the sound of someone whistling the tune of a now largely long forgotten pop song.

The song has been identified as "Comin' In On A Wing And A Prayer." Recorded by a group of crooners called The Song Spinners, it topped the Billboard Best Selling Singles Chart for three weeks in July 1943. (Frank Sinatra, Anne Sheridan, Gene Autry, Bing Crosby and Eddie Cantor also all cut versions of this song.) The lyrics – "tho there's one motor gone, we can still carry on" – made it a particular favorite of US airmen, and none more so than Eddie Slabaugh, who was once threatened with being suspended from duty on half-pay for whistling the tune during a mission briefing session.

Interestingly, the ghost that haunts the Thorpe Abbotts control tower is not a new phenomenon, as he first began to appear during early 1944, when he was reported being seen walking through walls of the airmen's quarters. Back then, men could recognize the ghost. And even if they couldn't recognize its face, they could certainly recognize the tune it was whistling. "Comin' In On A Wing And A Prayer."

Tales of the "Eddie the Ghost" persisted, with some of the men even taking their pistols and rifles to bed with them. Fearing an accident, the base commander at the time Colonel Thomas Jeffrey, known as Colonel Jeff, even banned all talk of Eddie on penalty of court martial.

Perhaps it would have been possible to lay to rest the ghost of Eddie Slabaugh if someone had remembered to carve his name on that war memorial in the old Salem Cemetery, but that opportunity was missed 70 years ago. Eddie the Ghost was whistling then; he's still whistling now.

~Charles Christian

Woman Hollering Creek

Soles against bank
Skirt billows beneath
Damp from heat
Tears, down her cheek

Hand to empty womb
Her child, glassy eyes
... breath still
Floats, beyond dawn

Murder, they whisper
Mother, daughter
He left town last month
Mexico bound for another

She haunts this watery grave
In wind, a mile past farm
Restless, as mosquito bite
Woman Hollering Creek

~JR Vork

Watching the Lamar River Rapids

I thought I saw a single drop
Lurch and hop across a rock
And wondered if he'd rather stay
To sun himself in sleepy thought.

I guessed he'd love to waste a day
Lurking in the marshy shade
And gazing out on rolling hills
That mark his lifetime's barricade.

Perhaps he'd scan the tranquil
Sky, as pudgy puffs of silk
Slink by, playing recluse
Cloistered by the wistful still.

But in my heart, I knew he would not choose
A path that strayed far from the rule
Or lose his place to others rushing through.
I watched and whispered - Yes, me too.

~Tovah Yavin

Springtime

arrived, open mouthed, black,
screeching harpy-like in the tree
branch above my picnic table, sure
to shit all over the white paint, something
dead hanging from her claws; mechanically

I open the window, remove
the screen, careful not to disturb
the beastly presence – ease barrels
one and two over the sill, silver
bullets prepped; cock, aim

feathers scatter to the ground, stick,
sprout, blossom as I watch – daffodils,
tulips, irises, lilies – the dead thing
scampers to freedom, a chill in pursuit,
as the bird silently changes colors: black
to blue to green to yellow to orange to
red to brown with a rainbow in the light,

a song emerging, slowly at first –
it has been a long winter; I'm ready,
as light glints off feathers, feet crouch
and spring is here again, skipping
across the grass, singing for worms.

~John Reinhart

Under The Stars

I

"Thanks for coming. I'm sure my father would have appreciated it." Robert forced his lips into a smile as the elderly couple made their way through the door. Norma and Gene Halloway lived next door, and had known Robert's father for twenty years. They'd stopped over after the funeral, plopped down on the couch, and proceeded to tell every story they knew about John Northrup. Robert smiled and nodded and refreshed drinks, stuck in his suit and tie until eight o'clock, when Gene stood and said they'd let him try to relax.

After the door was shut, Robert tore the tie from his neck and flung it onto the back of his father's easy-chair. He collapsed into the worn seat, the smell of his father wafting up from the faded corduroy, and propped his feet on the coffee table. If he'd been there, John Northrup would have cleared his throat and given him a look of disapproval, but he wasn't, and Robert was too tired to care.

Robert pushed the seat-back and threw an arm over his eyes. His suit jacket scrunched up between his shoulders. He knew he should get up, hang the suit and shirt, and get into something more comfortable, but now that he was lying down all the will to move drained from his body. "Screw it." He kicked off his shoes – a minor concession to his father's ghost – and waited to fall asleep. The sooner this day was over, the better.

He remembered his father's last call. He'd been hunched over his desk reading some bullshit memo when the intercom buzzed. The receptionist said it was his father, asked if he want to take the call.

"Robert? I need you to come down here." John's voice sounded far away and fuzzy, like he'd called from overseas instead of Indiana.

"Come down? Why?"

"I can't explain, Rob. It's important." The line hissed and came back. "Please, Robert."

He scanned the next week of his calendar and grimaced.

"I'm sorry, Dad. I have a huge deadline next week. Can it wait until after then?" Static filled the line for a long time. Then his father said "Forget it," and hung up.

Gene Halloway called a week later. John had been found in the garage. He'd hung himself.

Robert shifted in the chair. The half-empty bottle of bourbon still sat on the dinner table next to a thin manila envelope. He dropped the footrest and clambered to his feet, peeled off the jacket, and tossed it onto one of the chairs around the table. He rolled up his shirt-sleeves and poured a glass. Then he broke the seal on the envelope and dumped the contents.

Two scraps of paper slid out onto the dark wood. The officer had said they'd been found in his father's breast pocket. One he recognized; it was a piece of his father's stationary. The other was an old map, yellowed and ragged along the edges. Someone had highlighted a route, marked one end with an X, and drawn in another line labeled "Rt. 542".

Robert set the map down and unfolded the other paper. Four wavering lines of text were scratched along the top.

>   *Robert,*

>   *This map took me to the stars. I watched them for hours.*

>   *They're so pretty in the dark.*

>   *I wanted to show them to you. You can still see them, if you look.*

He sat there for a long time, reading the note over and over. He picked up the map and traced the highlighted line with his finger. Without thinking, Robert downed the last of his bourbon, grabbed his phone, and dialed. Candace answered on the third ring.

"Hey, sweetie. How are you holding up?"

"As well as I can, Dee. How's the trial coming?" He smiled, not wanting worry to show in his voice.

"It's going well. I still think Rick could have covered for me, though. There hasn't been anything he couldn't handle. I hate that you're down there dealing with this by yourself."

"It's ok. Really. You're just an associate. It's a miracle they let you go to trial." She sighed, and he could almost see her shake her head and roll her eyes.

"Rob, it's your father's funeral. That should come first."

"Don't worry about it. I'm alright. But something came up, and I need to stay a bit longer to take care of it." He was amazed at how cool his voice was.

"I thought you hired a lawyer to take care of everything?" A note of alarm crept into her voice.

"I know, but Dad left something. It might have something to do with why he--" Rob sucked in a deep breath and held it for a moment. "Anyway, I have to look into it. Just a day or two more."

There was a long pause on the other end, and then she said, "Okay, but don't be too long." Worry still filled her voice, but Robert relaxed. She had agreed. She wouldn't raise the issue again. Not until he got home, anyway.

"I won't be, love."

Two days later, Robert climbed into his father's old pickup and drove out of town. Within five miles, the road was swallowed by corn fields, broken only by the occasional house and outbuilding. He followed his handwritten directions until he saw the sign for Route 542 and turned off. The pavement turned to pitted gravel. Loose rocks rattled off the undercarriage, and he could hear the heavy grind of the wheels on the road. He watched for the sign marking Donovan's Way.

An hour passed along rolling hills and bad roads. Ahead, he saw a thick line of trees. The road didn't appear to turn. Twenty minutes later, he drove into a dim forest that showed no sign of ending.

I must have passed it. He checked the mirror. *I should just go back. What's the point? Knowing what's out here won't bring him back.*

He was so focused on whether to turn back that he almost missed the sign peeking out from behind a massive fir. He slammed on the brakes and turned into the skid of his rear tires.

The 'road' was little more than a pair of ruts cutting through the trees. Ferns grew between the tracks and obscured the way forward. Robert looked back the way he'd come, then down at the map clipped to the air vent. He swung the steering wheel over and turned in.

The cab filled with a hushed whisper of the undergrowth brushing along the doors. The truck lurched as he drove over shallow ditches and deep potholes. The X marked a spot just past a tight bend in the road, so when the tracks brought him through a sharp switchback, he slowed to a crawl and scanned the roadside.

Robert saw the trail just as he passed it. He pulled off the road and shut the engine down. After a long moment, he popped the door open and stepped out.

The air was still and warm on his face. Sunlight filtered through the trees, casting bright spots on the truck. A bird sang somewhere ahead, and the buzz of insects filled the air.

Robert reached behind the driver's seat and pulled out a battered red duffel bag he'd found in his father's broom closet. The nylon was tattered and stained black with oil, but the straps were sturdy enough to hold a flashlight and a few bottles of water. He stepped around to the back of the truck and stood at the mouth of the trail. It extended like a tunnel for ten feet before disappearing around a bend. He glanced back at the truck, dust-coated and battered, shook his head, and walked into the woods.

Within half a mile, the foliage around him grew so dense he couldn't see through the trees on either side of the path. It gave the impression of walking down a narrow hall with textured green walls.

Minutes stretched into hours, and the trail gave no sign of changing. It wound through the forest at a steady decline. Robert stopped and took a long drink while he turned to look back up the trail. It twisted its way uphill for twenty or thirty feet before curving out of sight.

What was he doing out here? He tried to imagine his father working his way through these woods. John Northrup had been sixty-seven when he died. He walked a mile a day, but this kind of trek would have been monumental. As it was, Robert's calves were sore, and there was no telling how much farther he had to go.

The forest grew dim and cold as he went. Robert's watch read just after one in the afternoon, but the mid-August heat had evaporated. He shivered and rubbed at his arms. There'd been a thick flannel jacket in the hall closet of his father's house, and he wished he'd grabbed it. His breath misted before his eyes. Still, it wasn't too bad as long as he kept moving.

His foot came down on a stick with a dry snap, and the sound echoed through the woods. Robert stood still, hearing nothing but his own heart pounding in his ears. When had it gotten so quiet? At the road, the woods had buzzed with the sound of birds and insects. Now, no matter how hard he strained, he heard nothing.

"What the hell?" He glanced down at his watch and his jaw dropped. The numbers flickered, flashing so fast he thought of the read-out on a gas pump.

It's time to get out of here. He turned, took one lurching step, and froze.

The trail wound uphill for another ten feet and disappeared into a wall of brush. A puckered line ran down the foliage where the trail ended like a half-healed scar. The only sound was his breathing.

By the time he turned back down the path, the puckered line was gone.

Robert found the clearing an hour later. Fading light slanted through the canopy, glittering off dust motes like snowflakes. Small piles of worn stones, pitted and mossy, were strewn about brown grass. Off to his left, a massive stone column lay broken on its side, enveloped by moss and vines. He scrubbed at his arms and sighed, spewing a jet of cold mist.

A gray spire of stone stood in the center of the clearing. Ancient carvings covered the surface, the angular marks worn away to shallow scars.

Robert circled the clearing. The trail didn't pick up anywhere, and by the time he circled back around, it was gone completely. Despite the cold, his back and armpits were clammy with sweat.

He circled the clearing again, spiraling closer to the center. He found a stone half buried among the ferns that had been hollowed out into a bowl. A narrow trench snaked through the vegetation from the bowl to the spire.

"Why did you come out here?" he whispered. He stepped closer to the stone spire. Deep pits marred the surface and disfigured the markings. He traced his finger over one of them and something...shifted inside.

Robert lurched back. Blackness seeped up to the surface like oil, filling every inch of the stone. The markings disappeared. Robert reached out and touched it. The stone was completely smooth, like polished onyx. A light flashed on the surface, and then another. Robert glanced at the canopy, expecting to see sunlight, but the sky had gone dark. He looked down and gasped.

Tens of thousands of lights shone out from the black stone. They looked like stars. Something thrummed inside. He felt it in his stomach like the low buzz of a bass amp and took a step back.

I don't care if the trail is gone. He took another step, eyes wide and frantic. *I'll run through brambles if I have to.* He tried to take a third step, but his leg was stuck. Something pulled at him—toward the stone. Robert locked his knees, whipping his head back and forth. His arm dragged up, palm out, and the pressure increased until his shoulder popped. He staggered forward until his hand met the smooth surface.

The lights swarmed to his hand. They pulsed with his heartbeat. A voice whispered in his ear. It spoke in guttural, unintelligible words. He grabbed his wrist, jerking on his trapped arm and wincing against the tearing pain in his palm.

Callused hands bit down on his shoulders and squeezed. He sucked in air to scream, but before he could utter a sound, they shoved him into the stone.

II

Candace drummed her fingers on the steering wheel and sighed. She'd been sitting outside the Arrivals terminal for almost an hour before Rob stepped through the doors with a red duffel bag slung over his shoulder.

His eyes widened when he spotted the car. He approached with his head down. Rob yanked the door open and slung the bag into the back seat. Candace flinched, the strap of the bag flailing past her face.

"Easy there!" She laughed and ran a hand through her hair. "You almost took my eye out."

Rob fell into the seat and pulled the door shut.

He said nothing, just sat there with one hand cradling his head. He didn't even buckle his seatbelt. Candace waited another moment, then started the car and eased away from the curb.

~~~OOO~~~

Rob bolted the second she pulled into the garage. By the time Candace shut off the car and climbed out, he was up the back steps and unlocking the door. She pulled his red duffel from the back seat and slammed the door. The bag was light and something clinked inside.

She got halfway to the back door and froze. *Where the hell is his luggage?* He'd left with his black nylon garment bag and a large, roll-on suitcase. She'd never seen this bag before. It smelled like old dust and motor oil. She bit her lip and peered back at the car.

Inside, Rob sat at the table with his back to her. She went around and sat opposite him. He didn't look up.

"What's going on, Rob?"

He squirmed in his seat and picked at the front of his shirt, but he kept his eyes fixed on the table.

Candace paused, bit her lip. "Did you find something?"

His eyes flinched. Candace wasn't sure what to say, so she said nothing.

"Please, Dee. Don't worry about it." Rob folded his arms over his chest.

"Don't worry?" Candace leaned forward over the table and held out a hand. "Rob, of course I'm going to worry. You just lost your father. You need--"

"I needed you there!" He slammed his palm on the table and Candace flinched back, jerking her arm to her chest. Now his eyes were fixed on hers; they blazed in his ashen sockets. Then they widened and dulled, and his mouth drooped. "Dee...I'm sorry. I didn't mean that."

"It's ok." She spoke in a dull monotone around short, quick breaths. She forced herself to take a deep breath.

"Dee, I'm exhausted." He came around to her, bent down and grabbed her hands. His skin was cool and clammy. "I'm sorry I said that. I love you. I know you had to be here. I just need some rest. I'm going to sleep in the guest room, tonight, ok?" He stood and turned toward the hall. "We'll talk in the morning, I promise."

A moment later, the door clicked shut. Candace let out the breath she'd been holding. She grabbed her keys and slipped out the front door. She needed to cool down, and a walk sounded perfect.

Candace woke with a jolt and sat straight up in bed. She reached for Rob, only to find a cold hollow where his body should have been. She sighed and pinched the bridge of her nose. The clock on the nightstand read just after four in the morning.

She swung her feet out of bed and crept down the hall to the guest bedroom. She couldn't hear anything through the door. She twisted the handle and edged it open. A faint smell drifted out, like dirt and decaying leaves. Rob sat on the bed, hunched over staring out the window. He muttered under his breath.

"They're coming. The stars." He rocked back and forth, shaking his head. "No. No, I can't. I *can't*." He stopped mumbling and she heard a dry snap, like a twig breaking underfoot. She took a step into the room and froze. She bit her lip and looked back to the hallway.

He promised we'd talk in the morning. She inched the door shut. A moment later she was back in bed, wide awake. She lay there a long time before sleep took her.

Candace woke with the sun beaming through the blinds. She rubbed her eyes and sagged back into the pillow. Her back ached, and her pajamas were sticky with sweat. She sighed and untangled herself from the sheets.

The guest bedroom was still shut. She tip-toed down the hall and eased the door open. All she could see of Rob was a tuft of dark hair sticking out the end of a mound of blankets. She watched him for a moment, then shut the door.

I need to clear my head. She changed, found her running shoes, grabbed the spare key, and headed out the door. The air was still cool, and she fell into a steady pace, focused on her breathing, her footfalls, her posture. Her mind drifted.

Three miles later, covered in a slick sheen of sweat, she rounded the corner onto her street with a smile. The first ideas of what to say when Rob got up had bloomed around the second mile, and now she was certain things would turn out right. The smile vanished with the roar of an engine and squealing tires. Rob's car ripped out of the driveway and jerked to a stop. The gearbox clunked, and he took off in a haze of smoke.

She sprinted the rest of the way home and found the note on the bed.

Dee,

I need to be away right now. It will be better for both of us.

I finally understand.

I love you.

She dialed his cell immediately. After two rings, she realized she could hear it buzzing in the guest room.

"Shit!" She ended the call and tossed the phone onto the bedside table.

The day passed in a blur of worried glances out the window. She called his friends. She called her mother. No one had seen him. She waited up as long as she could. When she woke, propped up on the couch with a sore back, she hauled herself to bed. She promised herself to call the police if he wasn't back in the morning.

III

Her alarm buzzed—it was still dark outside. The smell of dead meat rolled over her when she opened the bedroom door. She swallowed hard and covered her face with her shirt. The guest bedroom door hung open. She inched toward it but stopped when she reached the entry to the dining room. Rob sat at the table, his hands out of sight and his eyes closed. She heard a dry snap and his lips twisted— then he looked up.

Candace gasped and pulled her clenched fists tight to her chest. His eyes were dark gray pools set in milky yellow.

"Robert, we need to talk." It took every bit of effort she had to keep her voice calm. "I know you must be going through hell, but you're scaring me."

Robert said nothing.

She edged over to the table and sat across from him.

"Rob, please, talk to me. You don't have to do this alone." She held her hand out for his.

Robert stared down at her hand and grinned. Blood trickled between his teeth.

Candace gasped and pitched back in her chair. Robert brought his hands up and the reek of rotting meat filled the air. Jagged shards of bone jutted through the skin of his fingers. The fingertips dangled like ornaments. He shot out his hand and grabbed her arm. The bones jabbed into her wrist.

"There's something I need you to see." His grin widened, pulling his lips tight over his teeth.

Candace jerked her hand back and flung herself toward the hallway. Robert leapt to his feet and his chair clattered to the floor. He flexed his hands. They crackled.

"The stars are coming, Dee. Let me show you."

Candace backed into the hallway and forced her eyes away from his ruined hands. They fell on the lamp next to the bed. She turned, took two steps down the hall, and sharp fingers clamped down on her shoulder. She screamed and batted at his hand. Something heavy crashed into her head. She didn't remember falling. She looked up through a narrowing tunnel of black, and all she saw were those dark eyes blazing down from pools of yellow.

Candace woke in darkness with the smell of oil and gasoline in her nostrils. The world seemed to bounce and jostle. The roar of an engine filled her ears. A rag had been stuffed in her mouth, rough and oily, with a strip of tape holding it in. Her wrists were bound behind her back. She kicked and screamed until her throat was raw. She lay there, curled up as much as she could, sobbing and defeated. Exhaustion overtook her and she passed out.

She woke to the sound of a slamming door. Gravel crunched underfoot, she heard a jangle of keys, and then the trunk popped open.

A shadow moved in the dark. Sharp, grasping hands pulled her into the night air. The smell of rot was overpowering. She gagged and struggled to swallow, terrified of throwing up with that rag sealed in her mouth.

After the pitch dark of the trunk, her eyes drank in the starlight. They were on a narrow track with weeds growing between the wheel ruts. Trees loomed on both sides. She looked up and caught a glimpse of the stars through the canopy. Robert slammed the trunk shut and pushed her toward a small path, just visible in the gloom.

"Walk." Robert's voice was unrecognizable, dry and rasping. When she didn't move, he shoved her. The bones of his fingers jabbed into her back, and her skin writhed.

She walked.

The canopy grew dense and solid as they moved into the woods. Candace slowed to a crawl. She could barely see the faint outline of the trail. Robert grabbed her shoulder and pushed her along, turning her with sharp twists of his wrist. They walked like that for hours.

The trail led to a wide clearing deep in the woods. A smooth, black column stood at its center, gleaming in the pale moonlight. Stars reflected off its surface—no, not reflected—the stars shone out from inside.

She pushed back against Robert, ignoring the flare of pain as his fingers ground against her shoulder blade. Robert grabbed her and something jerked between her hands. The rag split. She reached up and tore the tape from her mouth and spat out the wad of greasy cloth. She took one step and then he shoved her to the ground. She flailed with sluggish, numb arms and crashed face-first into the dirt. Her forehead hit something hard and blood streamed into her left eye. She struggled to crawl.

Robert grabbed her by the arm and dragged her toward the spire. She saw a hollowed out stone, like a bowl, and then he flipped her onto her back. He knelt with his knee digging into her mutilated shoulder, and she screamed and thrashed under his weight. He set the red duffel next to her and pulled open the zipper. He pulled out a long, gray dagger. It was stone, chipped and marked. Candace's eyes went wide.

"Robert, no! You don't have to do this."

Robert nodded his head. "I do. You don't understand."

"No! You don't! Please, Robert. I love you. Don't do this!" Tears streamed from her eyes, dripping down into her ears.

"It'll be over fast, Dee." Robert smiled down at her with glassy eyes, still and unfocused. "Then we can be with the stars."

He brought the stone dagger high over his head, and she jabbed her free hand into his throat. His eyes popped in surprise and he fell back gasping for air. Candace scrambled to her feet. Robert looked up at her with a blood-soaked snarl. She took one step toward him, pivoted, and kicked him in the face. He fell back, insensate.

Then something came out of the woods.

It crept along on four writhing limbs. Candace stood, frozen in place, while it scuttled through the thick ferns and hauled itself upright on the spire. The stars drifted to its touch and it cocked its head sideways. Intent. Focused. The stone went black. It turned to look at her with orange eyes that glowed despite the dark.

When those eyes fell on her, Candace screamed. The cold air burned raw in her throat. Its mouth twisted into something like a grin—she spun and ran.

She was twenty feet up the trail when it crashed through the edge of the clearing behind her. It plowed through the brush in a cacophony of snapping branches and whipping leaves. Candace pumped her legs, kept her eyes fixed on the narrow strip of dirt in front of her, praying that it didn't disappear in a sudden turn. Her lungs burned from the cold. She heard ragged panting close behind her.

A root snagged her foot and she crashed to the dirt, pain flaring in her shoulder. She flipped and tried to bring her hands up. The thing scrambled up the path, less than five feet behind her. It dropped to all fours, creeping toward her in sudden, jerking movements. She clambered back, feeling for something, anything. Her hand brushed past a rock, then darted back. She jammed her fingers into the dirt, prying at the edges. It crawled over her, its face inches away. It reeked of stale sweat and dirt and old crypts. It grinned wide, revealing jagged teeth.

The rock came free.

Candace slammed it into the thing's head. Pain flared in her back, but it fell sideways, its arm pinning her to the dirt. She wriggled free and rose to her knees. She brought the rock down hard again. And again. It laid slack, its eyes open and unfocused, its head sunken and wet. She dropped the rock and sagged to the ground. She lay there, wracked by sobs and shivering. When it passed, she staggered to her feet and limped up the path.

~~~OOO~~~

By the time Candace stumbled back to the road, the horizon was a pink blister. Dew coated the car and dripped from the open trunk. She used the sleeve of her shirt to wipe the moisture from the driver's side window. Gelatinous black chunks filled the seat and a crust of dried blood coated the wheel. She sucked in a deep breath, covered her face with her shirt, and opened the door.

She spun and staggered off the road, expelling the thin contents of her stomach in rough heaves. When it was done, she took another deep breath and ducked her head into that reeking space. The keys were gone. She lurched back and slammed the door. She glanced up and down the road. It was nothing but two thin tracks heading in either direction. With a last glance at the head of the trail, she headed in the direction opposite car.

A farmer in a rusted pickup found her wandering, head down and shuffling, just after noon. She screamed and drew back like she'd been burned when he touched her arm. Thick scabs circled her wrists and dried blood blackened the shoulder of her shirt. He coaxed her into the passenger seat and drove straight to the nearest hospital.

The police found Robert's body four days later, slumped next to his car. His throat was shredded, most likely by his own finger bones, according to the coroner. The path into the woods died after thirty feet.

The hospital released Candace a week later. Her parents took her straight to the airport, and then to the house she'd grown up in. She slept in her old bed under faded posters and threadbare sheets. Days passed, turned into months. Details began to fade. The nightmares weren't so frequent. They only came on clear nights after the moon had set, when the stars shone down through her window.

~Joseph Benedict

Untitled Poems

I.

I'm as dark
as the dreams of a demon
cold to the touch
as if I'm already
partially dead
I stroll around in the shadows
dodging the sun
and the acceptable sanity
that governs them
most of them
there are others
hidden among the living
others of another world
chained by the gravity of this one

II.

You wander around
in the shade of my dark side
as if you're on safari
walking with wild things
along eroding edges
and living to tell
but we are not the same
and you were not invited
you are simply a tourist
exploring the zoo
pressing your forgettable face
up to the bars
of pacing and caged beasts
plotting their revenge
pacing and caged beasts
who would choose their own death
over being your display

III.

Self-perception
the confusion that binds mirage and reflection
a centaur that roams in the overlap
who I am to myself
is a movie based on actual events
filmed with a blurry lens
when all appeals are exhausted,
who I am to you, is who I am

IV.

I love most
people who are ferociously flawed
but flawless
in certain moments with me
I'd rather walk with the wounded
than dance with the divine
I can admire the soft light
of your purity
from any great distance
but it's your demons I want to kiss

~Bekah Steimel

Commuting

A day breaks
Unfettered by guilt
or gravity. The foothills
seem to be laying back,
reclining. The dirt
sighs, aware of the heat that will
return unabated. The water flattens
and seems to shutter in the face of the first light.
Receiving all kinds of waves, long and short,
and some that go right through it. I am
slowly putting on a shirt in the guest
room. Quietly moving to the door,
car, airport. So early that the
suburban sprinklers are just
starting their pre-programmed
cycles. And I can't tell if it is
morning or night.
The sky providing
No clues.

~*Morgan Bazilian*

Visiting New Places

The skies are purple
in Inwood...
an Indiana town.
where color is a bit off
on the common things...
a bit of a mystery the locals say

when passing through,
one sees a place a little touched
as if a sorcerer's wand misfired
just at the start of twilight
and the color held.

It makes just a little difference
but great beauty and merely pretty
are made by definition and even
the beholder can't answer why.

~*Lynette Esposito*

Silence

the birds are quiet
in Inwood Indiana
at dusk in summer

~Lynette Esposito

I'll Be Back

Death knocked on the wrong door,
twice this week.
He stopped on my street,
bold as a cloudless sunrise.

He checked his book,
across the road,
one door down,
slid on in.

The guy over on the
odd side of 40th,
one door down,
put up a fight, and,

Wouldn't die,
after the ambulance ride,
and emergency dance,
he came home still kickin,

Until last night when,
death dropped by,
gripping his lined, 3x5,
looking for the right address.

Mumbling, "This is the right street,
I know he lives here.
I saw him playing with,
His daughters' dogs."

He looked hard at my house,
he sensed me peeking back,
as I felt him looking, then,
went one door down across the street.

He took the guy this time,
and kept him.
Dead,
despite firemen, EMT's and cops.

You can hear death's thoughts,
when he comes for you,
And last night,
Death thought,

"This ain't right.
Paperwork's wrong but,
can't go back empty coffined.
Return trips are expensive."

~Timothy Philippart

The Drought in Wichita Falls

Some say the city will dry up
and be forgotten,
while others prefer
to keep quiet
and go about their days,
watering lawns at designated times
and displaying their faith
in the Good Lord with
signs petitioning
the Catholics and skeptics
to petition the Good Lord,
in his anger and wrath,
to show mercy
upon this patch of earth,
no less than three-quarters dirt,
where prayers escape
from a crack between the doors
of the church
to go and twist among the branches
of mesquite trees —
all thorn and no rose:
sharp reminder of Eve's curse
and the pang of hope
for Adam's redemption.

~*Samuel Underwood*

Inwood Knows

I.

Inwood knows

what it is to sleep
in a kill-zone, and
hear the trains scream
through the straggle
pines that we call

"The Woods".

Inwood knows

the first snowflake
on a steel-sky day.
The empty fields,
the empty air, that
only moves around trains.

Inwood knows

that a town can be
pride like a chipped
cookie jar--blue
Dutchware--roughed
up from handling.

2.

Inwood knows

that beneath blue oxen
and blue clocktowers
and little blue houses—
you may find cookies,
or the ashes of a man

Inwood knows

who died and was burnt.
Who made too much ash
for his beer stein
and so rests in his
mother's Dutchware.

Inwood knows

he chipped it with his
hunger for something
sweet and his clumsy
five-year-old hands.
The trains still move

Inwood knows.

~Stephanie De Haven

White Lies

Cassie tried to concentrate on the familiar scenery outside of the smudged, back seat window of her mother's clunky black '74 Impala. The same graying stalks of corn and the sagging wood of half-dead barns were flitting past as her mother flew down the winding country road. On either side, her five-year-old brother and two-year-old sister held fast to her hands. Mommy was raging at her from the front seat, but by now, at almost eleven years old, Cassie knew the argument was over when she stopped trying to make eye contact in the rear view mirror.

"Are you listening to me, Cassie?!"

"Yes, Ma'am," she mumbled.

"What did you say?" came back from the front.

Mommy's ranting died down and, with the exception of a few "dirty little liar" fragments, Cassie no longer heard anything she said. They slowed at the stop sign that separated the daily trip from the bus stop to the gravel road to their home. There was a white house on the corner—she liked to wonder about the people who lived there. *Were they nice? Did they have children?* She noticed the buck from their family of lawn ornament deer had been shot again. She hoped it was just a prank. *Who would shoot at their own lawn deer?*

At home, Cassie unbuckled her little sister from her car seat and cradled her in her arm while she gathered her book bag. Her brother didn't help much with anything. He followed his mother as if he were the only child. Once she was sure she wouldn't crush Becky's fingers or limbs in the heavy black door, she slammed it shut. She set her sister down, hoisted her book bag onto her shoulder, and extended her pinky finger for Becky to grab. They walked the gray slate slabs to the front door together.

Once inside, Mommy barked at Cassie to put Becky in the playpen and then to go to her room.

"Don't come out until I call you and you'd better have finished your homework by the time your father is home for dinner."

Yeah, yeah, yeah.

Cassie hadn't always minded being sent to her room. In their old house, she'd had her own room, with blue carpeting and pretty lace-curtained windows overlooking a tree-lined street. Now she shared a brown room with dirty-looking beige carpeting—and walls covered with dark paneling—and no real windows. Just like the rest of the trailer. It was divided by a homemade bookshelf that held her brother's toys. She stored her books under the bed.

Greeted by the cat waiting in the hall to follow her, she closed the door and flopped onto her bed. From her bag, she took inventory of the purchases she'd made at the school fund-raising bazaar. A red metal toy tractor for Rickie, $1.00; a soft little stuffed-animal kitten for Becky, $1.00; a seventy-five-cent metal measuring cup set for Mommy, who'd said you could never have too many when you were a good cook; and a wooden-handled pocket knife for her stepfather, Dave, $1.00. For herself, she'd gotten a *National Geographic* magazine from last February, 1980, for a quarter. Nothing else there interested her since they didn't have any real books. The total should have come to $4.00, and the change she'd gotten was a quarter. She hadn't looked at the receipt, hadn't questioned the eighth-grader at the cash register. Cassie had assumed the older girl was right. Her mother thought differently. She accused her of using the other seventy-five cents to buy herself some candy at a store near the school.

Cassie defended herself, saying she'd done no such thing. "Always so precocious," her mother said, "always trying to get away with things by blaming someone else." Cassie insisted on her innocence as long as there was still hope of using logic. But it brought a full-on storm of accusations, nasty words and, for Cassie, complete disbelief that a cashier girl, whom she didn't even know, could make this happen. Mother had railed about how selfish Cassie was, how much of a liar she was, and how piggish it was for her to buy herself candy instead of bringing home the change from the five dollars she'd been given.

Her mother's Siamese cat rubbed its face against her leg and mewed. Cassie placed the items in a row on the lid of the white wooden toy box at the end of her bed— *no one's interested in them now*—and pulled the cat up. She felt the rumbling of its purring and thought about her real father. She didn't know him—he'd left when she was just a baby—but she had a picture of him she kept in a shoe box with her memories. "Why are you yelling at her, Peggy?" he would've said, "Stop it! "

Cassie kicked off her saddle shoes and changed from her plaid uniform and white blouse to jeans and a t-shirt. She'd finished her homework on the long bus ride. Crouching on the floor to find a book, she decided on her favorites: *Jane Eyre* and *Wuthering Heights*. She'd read them both several times now, but still loved the passages that made her cry. She'd look at the engraved illustrations and pretend she was either Jane—"Forgive me! I cannot endure it—let me be punished some other way! I shall be killed if. . . "Or Cathy, "Hush, my darling! I'll stay. If he shot me so, I'd expire with a blessing on my lips." Or both. She might be Jane now, but maybe, someday, she could be Cathy just for spite. She opened *Jane Eyre* to the inside cover and traced her maternal grandmother's spidery cursive with her finger, "To Cassandra with Love on Her 10th Birthday – Grandmother." She turned the book over and picked up *Wuthering Heights*. Flipping through the pages, she stopped at the picture of Cathy sitting on a stone wall, her hair billowing in the wind, wild eyes searching for Heathcliff.

Dave came home with a bang of the front door and the cat bolted. Now that they lived in a trailer, you could hear just about everything. She listened to be called to dinner.

"Sueeey! Suey, suey, sueeey!" Mommy got a kick out of calling Cassie to dinner with a pig call.

Cassie, sighed, closed the book, and slid both volumes back under the bed. She went back down the narrow, linoleum-tiled hall in her sock feet to the dining/living room. In the old house they'd had a separate dining room. Everything had been so much bigger. But Dave had lost his job and the house had followed. He was working again, though the pay was far less, Mommy said. He was always in a bad mood when he got home. Before they'd had to move from the pretty house on Hill Street, he'd yell sometimes—usually a short argument between him and Mommy that had nothing to do with children, and one that ended in laughter. Now their arguments were in long, low growls and always seemed to be about her.

She squeezed into her chair at the table; it was, as always, immovably wedged against the wall. It was Chinese food for dinner. Mommy loved making Chinese food and, in the old house, it meant a special occasion. An occasion, for inexplicable reasons, that called for candle light so the family could play a game about making up what kind of bugs were in the stir fry.

Plates were passed, grace was said, and the meal began under the dusty white pendant lamp, like any other dinner. Mommy asked Dave polite questions about his day. Rickie was prodded to talk about kindergarten. When the conversation dropped off, Mommy turned to Cassie, eyes narrowed and sharp. "Tell your father what you did today." Her voice was too saccharine to be trusted.

"I bought everybody a gift at the bazaar and, instead of giving back all the change, I spent some of it on candy."

Mommy's jaw tightened. "What?" she hissed.

Cassie braced herself.

"You dirty little pig-faced liar," Mommy said, her voice a low, measured tone from between clenched teeth.

"Did you lie to your mother?" Dave demanded.

"No. Yes. I mean…I don't know!"

Cassie thought she was doing the noble thing by repeating her mother's version of events. Becky started wailing in her highchair, and Rickie fiddled with the napkin in his lap.

"It has to be one or the other, young lady. Either you lied or you didn't," Dave shouted.

Cassie had no idea what to say and thought about it a little too long. Dave was sitting to her left and smacked her head hard enough to hit the wall behind her. Stunned, she blinked hard. Becky was red-faced and howling now. "What do you have to say for yourself, young lady?"

Screw you. Cassie wouldn't have dared say those words out loud, even though she heard them at home all the time now. She stared down at her food and tried to imagine the varieties of gross things from the garden behind the house on Hill Street. *There are grasshopper wings, weird white worms, these mushrooms could be snails. Definitely lots of maggots involved.* She felt her mother staring at her and Dave quietly gearing up to give her another reason to answer more quickly. She lifted her chin and looked directly into his face. She was calm and confident when she spoke.

"I was given the wrong change for the stuff I bought at the bazaar today and Mommy didn't believe that I hadn't spent it. I didn't spend it. I didn't spend anything that I didn't bring home. I don't know why I got the wrong change. The girl who took the money was older than me so I thought I counted wrong. Mommy never believes me and I wanted to make her happy so I said what she said I did."

Cassie's mother's mouth dropped open and her face blushed as she shot her a dark look. "Since when have you ever wanted to make me happy? You're exactly like your father—you just make things up as you go along. You turn things around so you're never guilty. You think you can always come up smelling like a rose."

Cassie focused on the stir-fried maggots and pushed the wings and worms and snails around on her plate.

"A real pain in the ass, isn't she?" Dave forced a laugh and cleared his throat.

"And she'll end up with a really big ass, too, stealing money to buy sweets even when we feed her well enough, the little piggy," Mommy said.

Rickie giggled at the words "little piggy," and Becky stopped crying because Rickie was laughing. Cassie kept looking at her tainted food. Mommy and Dave went back to talking about his job and how stupid his boss was.

Cassie thought about the picture of her father. She'd stolen it from her mother's old photo album. He was sitting by a swimming pool laughing, a cigarette in one hand, a beer can in the other. The photograph was dated '71—ten years ago—but what month? Mommy said he went to Mardi Gras and never came back. But Mardi Gras would have only been during a February. She had read that in *The National Geographic*. Which February?

"May I be excused, Ma'am?"

"Not until you've finished everything on your plate, Miss Piggy," said Mommy, smiling at Rickie.

Cassie sat there, concentrating on her plate, trying to re-imagine it. *Rice...snow peas...bamboo shoots...water chestnuts...mushrooms...I like all those things. This is silly.* But she couldn't manage to do anything but push the food around on her plate. She couldn't erase the fictitious mess in front of her. When everyone else had finished eating, Mommy ordered her to leave her plate but clear the rest of the table, put Becky to bed, and wash the dishes. She and Dave lounged on the overstuffed couch and laughed at an old comedy on television. A couple of times Mommy ordered "Miss Piggy" to bring them a couple of beers.

It wasn't pleasant washing the dishes. Leaning her forearms against the edge of the sink, her mind wandered, and she imagined her father as an invisible witness. *He would shake his head with disapproval. He would take her face in his hands and tell her that it was okay that she looked like him. That he got lost on the way back from Mardi Gras but was coming back to get her soon. "Be strong," he would say.*

Dishes done, she dried her hands and asked for permission to go to her room even though her dinner still sat on the table. Her mother dismissed her drowsily—she couldn't drink more than one beer without falling asleep. But Dave said he had one more chore for her.

"We'll take out the trash together. Gather it up in the kitchen and I'll be right there."

Cassie knocked the kitchen sink's drain-catch into the garbage. Dave came in with her plate and scraped it into the bag without a word. He tied it up and pulled it from the can. She washed the plate, shook off the water, and put it away.

"I know all of this is tough for you," he said in a near whisper. "I'd really like to see what you got for everyone today. I know you weren't lying. When you said that you didn't spend the missing money on candy, I knew you didn't. Let's take out the trash. I want to show you something. Go get your coat."

Dave was sometimes nice after Mommy passed out. Cassie slipped past her mother and down the hall. There was a light snore coming from her brother's side of the room as she pulled on a jacket, slipped her sneakers on, and swept the gifts into her book-bag to bring with her.

In the kitchen, Dave had his coat on and the garbage bag in his hand. "Let's go," he said with a smile.

She followed him through the back porch that was the beginning of a house they were planning to build to replace the trailer—someday. Dave dropped the bag into the metal can, clapped the lid back on and motioned for her to come around the house and up the flagstones to his pickup truck.

"I just want you to know that you don't need to stay in your room all the time with the books you keep under your bed and the damned cat. I know it's tough for you. Your mother and I don't make it any easier. Shit, I was your age once. Nothing like you, but your age at least."

He leaned against the truck and pulled out a pack of cigarettes from an inside pocket. He lit one and inhaled. She didn't know that he smoked, and she doubted her mother knew either.

"You've got to get out and let off steam sometimes," he exhaled. "You know what I do?" He didn't wait for an answer. "I go hunting." Dave made air quotes when he said the word hunting and grinned. "Don't you ever tell your mother; she'd kill me."

He opened the passenger door for her to get in. Cassie pushed her purple backpack onto the floor and climbed up onto the seat, slamming the door behind her. Dave flicked the cigarette across the road, its red tip bouncing into the darkness. He drove in silence to the intersection at the end of their gravel road, stopping on the shoulder across from the white house on the corner—the one she passed on the way home from school every day. Its broken windows stared blankly at the lawn. She looked at Dave's face, lit up by the green of the dashboard light. The gold of his wedding band on the top of the steering wheel was caught by the headlights.

Gold. That's one of the colors of Mardi Gras.

"Don't worry," he said, "that house has been empty for years." Dave got out of the cab and pulled the rifle from behind the seat. Cassie remembered that he kept it behind the seat of his battered truck so it wouldn't be in the house—a safety measure, he'd said. He lifted it to his shoulder and took aim. The blast echoed as an antler on the plastic buck shattered. Cassie tucked her hands under her legs on the cold pleather seat and held her breath.

~Kristan Campbell

A Collection of Horror Story Haiku

Alone in the dark,
low chuffing in the tall grass,
which way did they go?

I fall from the bridge,
through memories toward my wife.
The coarse rope snaps tight.

Faint heartbeat chides me
eviscerating the air,
through worn gray floor boards.

Small town like Inwood
no one comes and no one goes,
not entirely.

You can feel the smell
of blood soaked into concrete
reverent butcher.

~Bobby Aldridge

The Bluish Hue

Midnight…I am doused in darkness, ignited in black suffocation… Yet I see an ethereal light?

With apparent reticence dawn arrives shackled to an impenetrable fog… Mother Nature has surreptitiously woven a blanket of blindness… Yet I see an ethereal light?

Stubbornly the fog dissipates and the cloudiest of skies emerge cloaked in shades of burnt charcoal… Yet I see an ethereal light?

Dusk arrives…formally announced by torrential rains. Tree limbs majestically bow to furious downpours, their leaves rhythmically detach, swirling in chaos… Yet I see an ethereal light?

Immersed within this ethereal light… haloed brushstrokes dabbed in hues of shimmering blue.

This ethereal light, it beckons me to a sanctuary… a spiritual haven, overflowing with love, compassion and peace. I am mystified by its seraphic blue hued streaks. I am embraced by a divine strength, yet haunted by an innate familiarity.

A sudden celestial tainted epiphany… This ethereal light? This bluish hue?

Undoubtedly it is my Mother's beautiful blue eyes looking down upon me… guiding me through life's darkest storms… gracefully leading me toward the light.

~Patricia Rossi

On Every Street

There's one in every town, an old house where an elderly person or couple have lived for years in relative isolation. The neighbors don't see them much and it doesn't appear as if they have any family or friends visiting them. On the rare occasions when they are seen, they may exchange a wave or nod at you as you walk past, but the message is clear: *I'd really like to be left alone, thank you very much.*

A young mother pushing a baby carriage may see a worn, gray-haired woman in a tattered bathrobe beckoning feebly from her living room window. What she is saying through the thick glass can't be heard, there are only jerky and insistent gestures, off-putting and awkwardly urgent. The young woman thinks *dementia* as she flashes a smile and nods at the grandmother before pushing on in a hurry.

At Halloween, children avoid the dwellings of the old and isolated, as do the Christmas carolers. When storms knock out electricity, few bother to see if the aged are all right or even if they have enough food. During heat waves, no one thinks to check to see if they have air conditioning.

The seasons are simply registered as changes in temperature for the elderly who live alone: it's hot for awhile and then cold, sweaters are worn and extra blankets are used for a few months, and then screens are inserted to allow in fresh air or a breeze when the sweltering nights arrive.

When an old person is no longer collecting their mail, only a few observant people notice. Unreturned phone calls are tolerated for a week or more, but after a month, the elderly need to be looked in on to see if they are all right. A grown son or daughter or other relative who hasn't visited in years will request a welfare check. The police will knock on the door and ring the bell and peer into the dirty windows. If there is no response, they gently gain access.

They are confronted with a sour stench. They track the odor to the back of the property. On the floor in the bedroom is the decomposing body of an old, withered up husk. The internal gases form large blisters, and the body has started to bloat and swell and leak.

Neighbors watch as a silent ambulance and a second police car pull up in front. In less than two hours, both vehicles have left as quietly as they arrived. The body is taken to the morgue and an autopsy performed the following afternoon. Yellow tape is stretched over the doors and windows, forbidding entrance.

A few days later, the tape is removed and a cleanup crew wearing protective gear arrives. They notice stacks of yellowed newspapers strewn about the rooms. Nothing appears to have been dusted or cleaned in many years. Flies now buzz about. After the bedroom is cleaned up, it's sprayed with insect repellent. Gloved hands empty the refrigerator of its long-spoiled food. All the garbage—nineteen bags—is removed and packed in the back of the truck.

They are finished in three hours. They make certain they've left none of their cleaning supplies behind. On the coffee table they place an air freshener. It has their company name stencilled on the bottom. Once they have checked to be sure all the doors and windows are secured, they say with satisfaction, as they always do, "It really doesn't smell that bad anymore."

Jeremy Jenkins, the nephew of the late Elroy Jenkins, arrived in town a few weeks after the cleaning crew left his uncle's home.

Nothing had gone right on this trip. Jeremy was late getting to the airport—he missed his flight. That had never happened to him before but the traffic to O'Hare had been worse than usual and, even though he had left in plenty of time, he was out of luck.

He waited three hours for the next flight to Akron. Because he had to rebook and the plane was almost full, he was stuck at the very back. His seat didn't recline. A storm blossomed out of nowhere and then went berserk, grounding all air travel for another two hours. When it was finally time to depart, everyone on board was in a foul mood and the crew matched each passenger's frustration, glare for glare.

Jeremy had booked the motel for one night. He had already contacted the real estate agent and planned to look at the house in the morning to see if he wanted any of his uncle's possessions—the realtor would meet him there at noon. This was not a trip of mourning; he had no sentimental attachment to the property or his uncle, whom he thinks he may have met sometime back in the 1980s. They never spoke on the phone or exchanged any letters. Elroy was one of his deceased father's seven brothers and Jeremy had no idea why he was the one stuck with his uncle's estate. It had all happened very quickly—at first, he was suspicious and thought it was a scam. *Who inherits real estate from a forgotten relative?*

But here he was, finding his way down the streets to his uncle's former home at 22 Mildred Avenue. The cab ride from the motel to this rundown area of town had been uneventful. The problem had occurred when the driver—brand new to the job, of course—hadn't known there was both an East Mildred Avenue and a West Mildred Avenue. He'd been dropped off at the wrong location. An exasperated call to the real estate agent cleared things up. He was five blocks shy of his destination.

Jeremy headed east and passed modest one and two-story homes, most of which needed a fresh coat of paint and serious landscaping. The further he walked and the more he saw, the surer he felt that he wouldn't be fetching much from Elroy's place. He would price it to sell, make a few bucks off of it if he was lucky, and consider it found money.

Clink, clink, clink.

Jeremy heard the sound to his left and stopped. He was in front of a two-story residence with a cracked "For Sale" sign planted in front of it, the handwritten phone number long ago bleached out by the sun. He remained still, straining to hear the sound again. It had been like metal tapping on glass. There was no one else around. He had seen three realtor signs and knew he'd be adding a fourth by the end of the day.

The sound didn't come back. Jeremy continued down the street, watching the address numbers descend as he moved down Mildred Avenue, until, at last, he was at his uncle's home.

It was a single story ranch that had once been painted brown; much of the color had chipped off or had faded over the years. A long stretch of elevated brickwork made up the face of the property. It held a tightly packed, robust cluster of weeds where Jeremy presumed flowers had once grown. Above that was a window. The lawn was yellow and weedy and the bushes were either dead or dying.

What a disaster, Jeremy thought. He wondered about his uncle, why he had spent his last years in this mess or why he hadn't bothered to maintain it. *And why give it to me? Were the other brothers dead?*

After his parents had passed away, Jeremy had no contact with the rest of the relatives. His father had come from a huge family of seven brothers and they were spread all over the country. They never seemed to have any money.

Jeremy dug the key out of his pocket, inserted it into the front door, and entered the gloom. The air was stuffy and heavy, the room freshener that had been placed on the coffee table had given up the effort; it was only a thin wedge of its former self. Jeremy flicked a wall switch. The weak bulb under a dust covered table lamp responded. It barely made a dent in the dimness. He could make out stacks of old newspapers that stood about him like sentries, but that was about it. Everything else was in shadows.

The kitchen was off to his right. In a few steps, he had moved from the patchy shag carpet of the entryway onto slightly sticky tile. His footsteps echoed for an instant, a hollow sound, and then all was silent. He parted the yellow, threadbare curtains that were above the sink. The glass behind them was filthy and smudged with fingerprints. Very little light came through. He unclasped the lock and struggled to open the window. He hoped the fresh air would usher out the odor.

Looking out at the back yard, he saw that it was much like the front; weeds, overgrown bushes, and a twisted metal fence. He saw a decrepit compost pile next to a stack of wood. That was it. No garden or any attempts at landscaping.

The refrigerator was empty and had been wiped clean. *Thank God.* Jeremy could only imagine what had been thrown out. One by one, he pulled open the drawers and scanned the contents: filthy, mismatched silverware; an assortment of rusty carving knives; a junk drawer; tools; rubber bands; ketchup and mustard containers from fast food restaurants; coupons that had all expired a decade earlier.

The cupboards were filled with the usual plates and pots and plastic containers. He checked the cabinets and under the sink. Nothing of value, nothing he wanted. The counters were covered with stacks of junk mail and catalogs. The calendar on the far wall was from five years ago.

Sad, Jeremy thought bleakly as he padded back onto the living room shag carpet.

He pulled back the drapes from the picture window. They released puffs of gray dust and debris. He stepped back while he watched them all settle. For some reason, the sunlight through the pane appeared greenish. He looked closer and discovered the glass was lightly tinted for privacy.

The living room had a sofa, a recliner, and a TV set in a cabinet. There were no photographs or any decorative items; it had even less charm than your cheapest motel room. The paneled walls and their vertical lines were everywhere he looked, somewhat like the bars in a jail cell. No bookshelves or posters or knickknacks or anything to show that someone had ever lived there.

There was an end table next to the recliner with two drawers. The top one contained a deck of cards strapped together with a rubber band and the other one was empty. A closet behind the recliner was filled with more stacks of newspaper. Jeremy had glanced at a few of the dates and headlines but it all appeared to be random, a collection from the past decade but gathered for no real reason that he could discern.

Sad, was the only word that again came to mind. Jeremy wondered about the tragic, bleak life his uncle lived. *What did he do here all day?*

The bedrooms were all that remained to explore. He hesitated because he knew that one of them was where Elroy's body had been found. Also, it was the most personal and private place in anyone's home. *I wouldn't want someone snooping through mine*, Jeremy thought. And he didn't really want to know anything intimate about his uncle. He was there to give the place a quick once over, check for any treasures, and then get it on the market and get it sold.

However, he supposed if there were any valuable items, they'd be in his uncle's bedroom so he started toward the hallway. But after only a couple steps, he stopped short.

There was something about the passage that made him hesitate. It looked unnaturally dark, as if it was closed off from the rest of the room, or wanted to be its own separate place, impassible.

Why would you think that? Jeremy asked himself even as he found he couldn't help peering into the deep blackness before him, trying to discern if there was anything he could see. Maybe all the windows in the back of the house were closed off or the doors were closed? The weak radiance from the lamp didn't stretch very far, and actually stopped at the corridor as if it had encountered a barrier.

He felt something shimmer off the back of his neck. He flinched wildly and cried out, thinking it was an insect, but realized it was just nerves.

Why am I so jumpy?

He squinted again into the deep gloom. Surely he was mistaken, but it seemed that the passage way was actively opposing any attempts of light to pierce its realm. He shook his wrists and squared his shoulders, trying to get himself energized. "Get a move on," he said, hoping his own voice would embolden him. But he sounded nervous and uncertain, and remained where he was. The longer he stood there, the darker and thicker the area before him appeared to be. He wanted to check out the bedrooms and then get out, but some creepy stupor had taken over.

Put some light on the subject—the thought came suddenly to him. He pulled his phone out of his back pocket. It was 10 a.m. He sighed with relief as he activated the flashlight app. The bluish-white glow burst forth like headlights or a flashbulb, and Jeremy was blinded for a moment. But it was powerful enough that the darkness fled in an instant. He was relieved and immediately calmed to see that it was just a hallway. *What else would it be?* he chided himself nervously. It was only about six feet in length with a right turn at the end where the bedrooms and a bathroom would be.

Jeremy kept the phone up in front of him as if it was a torch. The rug in the passage was thick and surprisingly plush for being so old. Another step and the shag carpeting was even fuller now. Suddenly, he felt his shoes sink into it, as if it was some type of moist sludge. *I bet the house flooded and the carpet is soaked through*, he thought with disgust. He lifted his right foot but the flooring maintained its grip, even tightening. Jeremy turned the phone to his feet. He was startled to see that the rug was dry. It was old and threadbare, not plush or water-soddened like he had imagined. With the illumination exposing all these facts, Jeremy lifted his foot easily. His hand was trembling and the light flickered about in the darkness as if trying to find an object to focus on.

Then it dawned on him: The place was probably stuffed to overflowing with that toxic mold that was poisonous, the stuff that made you hallucinate. He'd heard about it on one of those ghost hunter shows. They said that older buildings where hauntings were reported often had poor air quality from pollutants. People claimed they saw ghosts and demons. The fungi affected the brain and could cause psychoactive effects like people experienced when smoking mushrooms.

Jeremy thought this through. It all made sense. If he was already experiencing hallucinations after less than thirty minutes inside, then he shouldn't stay much longer. Fifteen minutes max. He thought it might be best to leave and get some fresh air. When he was ready, he could return to the bedrooms for a quick check of his uncle's possessions.

That plan made sense. He switched off the phone light and turned around.

"No way."

The living room wasn't there. Instead, there was an impossibly long passage, at least twenty feet in length, with a large picture window at the very end.

"That can't be possible." He squeezed his eyes closed and clenched his fists. When he looked again, it was worse, like gazing down the wrong end of a telescope.

Everything was now smaller and further away than it had been before. Panicking, and knowing he had to get out at once, Jeremy pocketed his phone and put his hands out in front of him. He moved toward the front of the house. Even if he was imagining all of this, he knew he was headed in the right direction.

The front of his head banged against a wall. Startled, he stopped and backed up. The back of his head gently tapped against something equally solid. He felt around in the dimness and touched…the ceiling. It was sloping down and he could not walk forward.

My mind is playing a trick on me but I can go along with it, he thought, even as his breathing changed to fast bursts of terror. *I just need to focus on reaching that picture window and the front door. That is real and that is where I must go. The house is not shrinking around me…*

He hunched over and began to scuttle quickly forward, gasping and whimpering. It was as if he was in a race against the house. The finish line and freedom waited at the front door. He moved as quickly as he could, his arms out like a blind man as he pushed on, until, without warning, he rammed both his shoulders between the walls. The hallway had abruptly narrowed.

For an instant, he was stuck. He squirmed around and then hunkered down further—he had to crawl on his hands and knees—his breaths now huge, unsteady gasps. He made slow, fumbling progress. He could see the window moving nearer and nearer to him. Sweat burned as it ran into his eyes so he closed them. He didn't need to see where he was going; he could only go forward.

Then, all at once, he reached the living room. There was the lamp with its dreary yellow glow. The recliner facing the TV set, the end table, the stacks of newspapers. It was all familiar and somehow comforting. If he had been able to stand, it would all have been normal, but he had to remain on his hands and knees. Even if it was only a hallucination, the ceiling still felt as if it had descended.

He was drenched in perspiration and his hands and knees felt burned and raw. He decided to rest for a moment. He wondered how much longer the illusion would last, how much toxin had he inhaled? What time was it? The real estate agent was due there at noon and when she arrived—

His cell phone.

He could call the realtor and tell her that he was tripping badly, that he had been exposed to a mighty powerful toxin and he needed to be rescued *How could he have forgotten his phone?* His head was pounding hard and he was finding it difficult to breath. He knew he was panicking so he forced himself to take slow, measured breaths.

In the confined space, he wasn't able to turn completely around; he felt like an animal in a cage. The phone was in his back pocket. He strained and twisted about to reach it. It was snug and tight and he concentrated on easing it out, inch by inch.

Then, from the hallway far behind him, Jeremy heard a rustling, like calloused hands being rubbed together for warmth. There was a muffled silence followed by a low-pitched chittering noise. It reminded him of the cheerful greeting a dolphin made, but then it sounded like teeth clacking together with a growing momentum.

From a different area of the darkness, the cries were repeated as if one thing was responding to another. Then a chorus of shrieks rose up and Jeremy had an image of dozens of bats fluttering into wakefulness. He swallowed hard. He heard moist suckling noises, then scratching sounds as if things were getting a grip, finding a foothold, preparing to launch.

His mind created horrific images of giant insects with human eyes, rodents that resembled gargoyles, sharp, blood red talons that loved to tear at flesh—he couldn't stop himself from imagining the worst.

Stop it, he told himself. *It's not real. Focus on making the call.*

He placed his thumb against the phone to unlock it, but it was oily with his sweat and the phone wouldn't accept his fingerprint. Behind him, he felt the air pressure change as the things began to advance. Their chattering and the sickening sound of their legs scraping against the walls terrified him.

The phone finally unlocked, and at the same instant, a movement outside caught his eye. Jeremy squinted and could see an elderly man leisurely pushing a baby carriage. He was a plump fellow with suspenders arcing over his shoulders. *A grandfather and grandchild, one generation following another.* If he could only get his attention...

He scurried quickly over to the window, painfully bruising his shoulders. He frantically began tapping the phone against the pane.

Clink, clink, clink.

Outside, the old man stopped pushing the stroller and looked toward the property.

The dutiful grandfather noticed a flutter of movement through the tinted living room window. He saw the outline of a man, crouched over, and he seemed to be gesturing to him. He was tapping something against the glass. The movements were jerky and insistent gestures, off-putting and awkwardly urgent. After a few seconds, the grandfather abruptly turned away. Something about that man in the window was disturbing. He needed to get his grandson back for his nap. The elderly man cried out, "Zoom!" and pushed hard on the handles as the baby giggled with delight.

Inside the house, Jeremy continued to frantically tap against the glass as the grandfather and carriage moved rapidly out of sight. Then, from the darkness behind him, he heard the wet, saliva sound of many lips being moistened, and the low growl of countless appetites preparing to be satisfied.

~Jeff C. Stevenson

Bobby Boyd's Bad Eyes

"A pony that can play poker? Bullshit!"

"I swear, Jennie, I seen it with my own eyes. Bobby trained it to play. And the scary thing is, it's good."

I shook my head as I crumpled a greasy paper napkin and shoved it into a greasier paper bag. I belched, wrinkling my nose at the smell of the chili dog and onions I'd just eaten. "I've got to get back to work."

My cousin Israel stood and followed me to the garbage can in the parking lot of Moo Chow's. I always thought it sounded more like a Chinese restaurant than a burger stand, but that's what it was—the only one in our little town.

He pushed in the plastic flap on the container so I could throw away the remains of our lunch. We had performed this ritual every Wednesday for the past two years, ever since I'd graduated from college and gotten a job at the library down the street.

I had been a good student, naturally smart, but impatient with puffed-up professors and clueless advisors. Turns out the advisors weren't *that* clueless, but I didn't realize it until I tried to find employment with a bachelor's degree in medieval literature. Six months into a fruitless job search, one of the ladies at the library retired.

When I wasn't surrounded by books, I partied with my cousin and our friends.

"You want, I'll ask Bobby if you can sit in on one of our poker games. You know how to play, don't you?"

"Ah, hell, you know I do, Izzy."

My daddy didn't teach me much before he took off for good, but he did show me how to play cards. Mostly because he knew it would piss off my mother. Mom's church didn't believe in cards. Or drinking. Or dancing. Or having fun of any kind. Probably why she didn't care too much for me. I *am* my father's daughter.

Izzy said, "Bye," and went inside Moo Chow's to finish his shift. I strolled down the sidewalk, pondering the idea of a poker-playing pony.

Saturday afternoon rolled around and my cousin called to invite me to poker night at Bobby Boyd's place. A few hours later, I found myself in the passenger seat of Izzy's jeep, trying to keep track of where we were going.

After we turned off the four-lane about ten minutes outside of town, we climbed up and down mountains full of curves. I thought I had been all over the back roads around home, but now I learned different. Bobby lived down a deep holler, just a narrow slit between two steep ridges. Hemlocks and pine trees crowded the sloping earth, casting long shadows across his solitary house.

"Bet this holler don't see the sun much," I said.

"No, and it's a real bitch in winter." Izzy shifted gears and guided the vehicle down the rutted road.

Once I bounced right off the seat and hit my head against the door. "Ow!"

"Sorry." We pulled onto a mossy spot at the edge of the yard and Izzy cut the engine. I surveyed our surroundings as the car *tick-tick-tick*ed in the cool air.

The house was nothing special. Probably built in the sixties—it was a little run down. Its white paint was peeling and it looked like it needed a new roof. The yard was clean, though, and rimmed by three small buildings in various states of decay. We got out of the jeep and walked through the grass to the front porch. That's where I got my first look at Bobby Boyd.

He sat in a wooden swing, dead center, his arms stretched out across the back of it. The ragged hem of his faded jeans brushed the floor of the porch as his bare feet kept the swing in motion. He wore a black t-shirt with a picture of Johnny Cash flipping somebody the bird. He was listening to the conversation of two men perched on the porch steps, one corner of his mouth turned up at something one of them had said.

We stopped at the bottom of the steps. Izzy nodded at the men. "Cal. Dennis." He cleared his throat and lifted his hand to the man in the swing. "Bobby, this is my cousin I told you about, Jennie."

Bobby stopped swinging and turned his head to look at me. His hair just touched his shoulders. Picture a jar of homemade apple jelly sitting in a sunny window. That was the color of his hair. But his eyes were dark.

Gypsy eyes—bad boy eyes—I knew I wouldn't be going home that night.

Bobby leaned forward and rested his arms on his knees. "You the girl wants to see my pony play?"

I nodded.

"Well, hellfire. Let's get this game going."

I had to apologize to Izzy for doubting him. Sure enough, that pony could play.

His name was Molasses, and that's what color he was, although his mane was as black as Bobby's eyes. He stood just outside the back of the house with his head poking through an open window. We sat at a round table pushed up against the wall. When it was Molasses' turn to play, Bobby would hold the cards up to him and he would nuzzle one to throw down. Every so often Bobby would feed him an apple slice or a baby carrot from a bowl under the table.

Now, a poker-playing pony is an amazing sight, but one that wins the game? I have to say, it was a little humbling. I'd never been a great poker player anyway, so I took it all in stride. Cal, on the other hand, got really mad. He had laid out a full house, sure that he had the winning hand. When Bobby showed the table Molasses' straight flush, Cal turned as pink as a cat's tongue. He cussed and shoved his chips across the table. One bounced up and hit the pony on the muzzle.

Bobby came across the table at Cal. The man would have gotten a beating for sure if Izzy and Dennis hadn't pulled Bobby off him. That kind of put a damper on the whole proceeding, so Dennis and Cal struck out for home. Izzy made out like he was leaving too, but I hung back.

"I'll bring her home," Bobby told him.

I could see Izzy wasn't comfortable leaving me there, but I didn't care. I grinned and waggled my fingers at him. *Hit the road, Cuz!*

I watched the jeep's taillights disappear into the darkness. I stood on the porch listening to the crickets. The sound washed over me, followed by a tidal wave of despair. For a moment, I felt the urge to run up the long, rocky driveway shouting, "I changed my mind, Izzy!"

The moment passed, and I returned to the living room. It was empty now. I kicked off my sandals, feeling the need to muffle my footsteps. I heard glass clink in the next room and followed the noise.

Bobby stood at the kitchen counter pouring Jack Daniel's into a shot glass. He tossed it back, then splashed some more into the glass. He held it out to me, a wicked form of communion I had taken many times, but never with such reverence as I had that night.

I crossed the room and pulled it from his hand. I turned the glass this way and that, staring at the amber liquid within. Usually I drank whiskey fast, but not this time. One slow swallow left a burning trail in my throat. I savored the fire, lifting my chin when I saw Bobby appraising me.

I looked around the room. It was messy. He had stacked dirty dishes in the sink. Empty beer bottles lined the backsplash. There was not a free spot to be found on the kitchen table; it held half-empty containers of pickle relish and ketchup, wrinkled potato chip bags, a crumbled pone of cornbread, and the remnants of a meal eaten hours ago. Bobby touched the nape of my neck and I shivered.

He pulled me close and ran his hands up inside my shirt, his calloused palms rasping my spine, filing me down to the core. I kissed him hard. A moment later we were groping each other, exploring new territories. Strangers in strange lands.

I stepped back and bumped the table. An open bag of cornmeal tipped over and dusted the vinyl floor. I curled my toes in the meal, surprised at how soft it felt. Bobby pulled me to the floor. We made love in a bone-white haze.

I woke up in the grey dawn and turned over in bed to stare at Bobby, who was snoring softly into his pillow. He looked different with his eyes closed, almost angelic. I would come to know better.

After rising from the bed, I grabbed a quilt from a nearby chair and wrapped myself in it. I walked through the house and stepped out onto the porch. Perching on the porch rail, I leaned my back against a post. I closed my eyes and heard two mourning doves call to each other. *I hope they find each other*, I thought.

After he got up, Bobby cleaned the mess in the kitchen, then fixed breakfast. Later I helped him feed Molasses, then we walked around the property. The best of the old buildings was a makeshift garage. It protected a Dodge Challenger, pitch black, like Bobby's eyes at night.

The second building was piled to the ceiling with junk. Moldering boxes of Reader's Digest magazines, rusty tools, and a broken hobby horse. I wrinkled my nose, then sneezed. "What are you doing with all this junk?"

"It ain't mine. It was here when I moved in."

"How long have you lived here?"

"Eight months."

I found out later that he had been raised on the other end of the county, on the border of Kentucky. That explained why our paths had never crossed before the poker game.

As we approached the third building, he took my hand. "We don't go in here."

"Why?" The building was the smallest of the three, low to the ground, but it didn't look like it was going to fall in anytime soon.

The door was held shut with a piece of wire. He unwound it and gave the door a shove. I saw a mound in the dim space, but couldn't make out what it was.

"It's an old cistern. The cover is broke. I guess whoever owned this place built this shed around it to keep people from falling in."

I hugged myself. "Kinda creepy."

"Yeah. I shined a light down there once. Couldn't see the bottom. I don't think there's much water in it. Smells awful. Probably ain't been used in fifty years."

He closed the door and tied it shut with the wire. As we walked back to the house, I couldn't keep from glancing over my shoulder at the cistern building. It made my skin crawl.

We spent the rest of the day in bed. I moved in with Bobby the next weekend.

The first three months were good. We both worked hard, me at the library and Bobby in his job as a coal truck mechanic. We played hard, too.

We christened every room in that house, and when the novelty wore off, we moved our lovemaking outside. I'm sure poor Molasses didn't know what to think when he saw us. There was hardly a tree trunk or tuft of grass that we didn't defile.

Of course, that biscuits-and-gravy kind of life didn't last long. Bobby lost his job in October. One rainy afternoon, after dodging puddles and swirling leaves, I entered the house and found him brooding in the kitchen. A bottle of whiskey stood on the table.

"What's wrong?"

"Laid off." He swayed in his chair. "Not much coal moving out of Virginia, so they don't need as many coal trucks. Or coal truck mechanics."

I knelt on the floor and wrapped my arms around his waist. My head rested against his chest. I felt his hand heavy in my hair. "You'll find something else."

But he didn't. A month passed, then another. There simply weren't any jobs to be had. We talked about him opening up his own garage, but neither of us had money to start a business. I dreaded the day his unemployment benefits would dry up. He was moody—any discussion of money led to a fight.

We had argued before, but never like this. I wouldn't say it out loud, to anybody, but his true temper scared me. His eyes were a mean kind of dark when he went into one of his rages. He'd scream at me, and throw things across the room.

After they repo'd his car, he broke half the dishes in the kitchen. He only stopped when a plate shattered against the refrigerator and a fragment hit me in the face. When he saw the rivulet of blood rolling down my cheek, he came to himself. He must have said he was sorry a hundred times that night.

"Sorry." It turned into a vocal tic.

"I'm sorry I kicked in the television screen."

"I'm sorry I threw your clothes in the yard."

"I'm sorry I hit you."

Yeah.

I think his apology was sincere the first time he did it. Truly. After I came out of the bathroom, eyes red and swollen from crying, I found him sitting on the top porch step. His head hung almost to his knees.

"I'm sorry, Jennie. I didn't mean to hurt you. I love you."

I dropped down on the step and peered at him. It was the first time he had ever said he loved me, although I had said it to him plenty. Without thinking, I popped soft kisses all over his face, as if my lips could erase his haggard expression of guilt.

But the more he said "I'm sorry," the less it meant.

I stopped having Wednesday lunches with Israel because I didn't want to face his questions. I avoided my friends, and withdrew from my coworkers at the library. I was ashamed that I had become *that* kind of woman.

You know the kind I mean. She "trips" on the stairs more than the average person. Has a lot of weird "accidents." Runs into doorknobs with her face. Wears sunglasses and scarves, not because she's stylish, but to hide the bruises.

But, finally, I found my last straw, the proverbial one that broke the camel's back. Or, in this case, the pony's back.

I came home one bleak February afternoon to the sound of Bobby screaming at someone behind our house. The fury in his voice was punctuated by an ellipsis of short, sharp thwacks. I ran around the corner of the house and found him beating Molasses with his belt. He was using the end with the metal buckle on it!

The trembling pony shook his head as if hornets were stinging him. He tried to back away from his master but Bobby had slung a nylon rope around his neck so he couldn't escape. When he lifted his arm to hit the pitiful creature again, I screamed, "Stop it! What are you doing?"

"Sonuvabitch stepped on my foot! Like to near broke it!"

His belt made a terrible sound as it came down on the pony's back. *Whup! Whup!*

I shoved Bobby away from Molasses and threw my arms around the animal's neck. "You know he didn't mean to do it! Don't hurt him!"

"Move, Jennie! Or I swear I'll beat you too!" His eyes were dark and flat.

"No," I said in a voice hoarse with fear.

He raised his arm and the belt licked the air before the buckle landed on my face. Feeling the skin tear, I screamed and fell to the ground at the pony's feet. I lifted my arms to protect my head from the next blow but it never came.

I heard the *thunk* of the buckle as the belt hit the ground. Bobby said in a dull voice, "I'm sorry." He turned and walked into the house.

I lay on the ground a long time with my hands pressed to the gash in my face. When I felt the blood begin to freeze on my skin, I got up. I ran my hands down the pony's back, weeping when he rolled his eyes at me, as if I might hurt him, too.

I led the pony to the empty garage. We had moved him there for the winter. After filling his water and food buckets, I rinsed the wounds on his back. We didn't have any kind of medicine, so I wasn't sure what else to do for him. I stroked his face, then walked back to the house. On the way there, I saw the belt, stiffening on the ground like a dead snake. I grabbed it and carried it inside.

Bobby sat in the living room staring at the broken television. He didn't look at me as I walked past him into the kitchen. I grabbed a bottle of whiskey and took a sloppy swig before going to the bathroom to check the damage to my face.

It was bad. I should have gone to the emergency room and gotten myself stitched up, but I didn't. I poured half a bottle of rubbing alcohol in it, biting my knuckles to keep from screaming at the pain. I laid a clean washcloth against it until the burn faded to a dull throb.

Returning to the kitchen, I drew a glass of water, then rummaged through the cabinet drawers. Bobby had hidden a bottle of prescription pain killers in one of them. He thought I didn't know he was using, but I wasn't stupid. When I found it, I popped off the cap and swallowed a pill with some water.

I shook the rest of the pills into my hand. Only four left, not enough to overdose. Glancing over my shoulder, I saw that Bobby hadn't moved. I stepped farther into the kitchen where he couldn't see me. Grabbing a can of green beans from a cabinet, I used it to crush the remaining pills.

I poured two fingers of whiskey into my water glass and set it on the table. After scraping the pill powder into my hand, I sprinkled it into the bottle, capped it, and shook it vigorously. Holding it up to the light, I examined it. It looked a little cloudy, but in the state he was in, he probably wouldn't notice. I carried the bottle and my glass to the living room.

"Here," I said as I handed him the bottle. "I think we both need a drink."

He stared at my face as he took the Jack Daniel's from me. I half expected him to say he was sorry. Instead, he lifted the bottle and took a long swallow. I sipped my whiskey and watched him over the edge of my glass. My heart skipped a beat when he grimaced, but all he did was wipe his mouth with the back of his hand.

"I love that pony. You know I do, right?"

"I know, Bobby." My voice sounded tired.

He nodded and tipped back the bottle again. This time he chugged it, as he was in the habit of doing when he was in a blue funk. I had banked on that. I finished my drink and set the glass on the coffee table. Leaning back, I covered my eyes with the back of my arm and waited.

I dozed off once, then jerked awake at the sound of the empty bottle clattering on the floor. Bobby had listed to one side, arm hanging over the side of the ratty old chair he favored.

"Bobby?"

He didn't answer.

I moved to him and shook him hard. He didn't respond. Crouching next to the chair, I laid my head against his chest. His heart beat slow but steady. His breathing was shallow.

"Bobby!"

Still he didn't answer.

I rose and padded to the kitchen. I retrieved his belt which I had laid on top of the refrigerator. Returning to the living room, I stood behind the chair and stared at the top of his head. I laid my hand there for a moment, remembering all the times I had clutched his long hair when we made love.

"I'm sorry, too, Bobby."

I threaded the end of the belt through the buckle then dropped the leather loop over his head. I pulled it tight around his neck. He didn't move.

I pulled it tighter.

He snorted, then gasped but didn't awaken.

I pulled it tighter.

His body knew something was wrong then, even if he wasn't awake to realize it. He started to buck in the chair, his hands flailing the air, his feet beating the floor.

Holding the end of the belt with both hands, I dug my feet into the base of the chair. I leaned backward and let the belt support the full weight of my body. I heard sounds...thick, wet sounds...but I didn't stop. Even when the chair started to tip over on me, I didn't stop.

When it landed on my legs, I let go and pushed the piece of furniture off me. I crawled to Bobby and rolled him onto his back.

His face was purple. The tip of his tongue poked out from his lips. He looked like an overripe plum that had split its skin. The worst part was his eyes. They looked like two pieces of coal embedded in dough.

Hanging onto the couch, I pulled myself to my feet. I don't remember what I did for the next few hours. I think I stared at the wall for a while. Then I doctored my face some more. I must have wandered from room to room in a daze. Finally, though, I came back to the here-and-now with the full realization of what I had done.

I had to take care of Bobby.

I stripped a quilt from the bed and rolled his body onto it. He had started to stiffen so it was an awkward affair. I pulled him out the front door. His head made a *bonk-bonk-bonk* noise as we descended the porch steps. I laughed and had to clamp it down tight for fear I wouldn't be able to stop.

It took me about twenty minutes to drag him across the frozen grass to the little building that sheltered the old cistern. The temperature had dropped with the sun and I had to stop every few feet to blow warm breath on my fingers. My face was numb, but that was a good thing. I couldn't feel the laceration now.

My plan was to throw his body down the cistern hole, then clean up all evidence of what I had done. I would tell everybody that he took off in the middle of the night.

I unwound the wire that held the door shut, then pulled it open with some effort. The sound it made as it scraped the frozen ground set my teeth on edge. I couldn't see a thing inside the building. It was as dark and cold as midnight can be.

I ran back to the house and grabbed a flashlight. When I returned, I pulled the body into the building. I shined the light into the cistern. I couldn't see the bottom. I ran my hand back and forth along the ground until I found a pebble, which I dropped into the hole. I didn't hear a thing.

The lip of the cistern wasn't high, so I didn't have much trouble lifting the body over the edge. I gave it a shove, and was shocked when I found myself falling alongside it. The flashlight cord, which I had wrapped around my wrist, had gotten snagged on Bobby's clothes.

We hit a thin crust of ice, then sank into dank water. His body broke my fall, the only good thing he had done for me in recent months. When the cold water seeped into the wound on my face, I screamed.

I fumbled for the flashlight, and though it had betrayed me earlier, it still worked. I moved the light up and down the walls of the cistern. It had been built better than the broken cover. Built to last. The stones were set together tight—no place to get a handhold. Even if there had been, the walls were covered in a film of icy slime. Slicker than snot on a porcelain doorknob.

I don't know how long I've been down her—maybe minutes—maybe hours. I'm not sure how much longer the flashlight batteries will last. Longer than I'll need them, I guess.

This water is so cold. If I didn't have ice water in my veins before, I sure do now. I can't feel my legs. My teeth are chattering so hard I'm sure the enamel is coming off them.

It's funny. I know I'm going to die here, but my mind keeps turning to the pony. Poor Molasses. He'll probably starve to death before anyone comes looking for me. I hate that.

I'd always hoped to see him get a royal flush when we played poker.

I think I'm going to turn off the flashlight now. Every time I shine it in Bobby's direction, the light glitters in his eyes. They got the best of me—Bobby Boyd's bad eyes—gypsy eyes—dead eyes.

~Neva Bryan

Journey Alongside a Minor Highway

People get swallowed
by sights and sounds,
unknowingly digested
by the world.

There are ways to escape,
to go higher, to be more
than indoctrinated particles,
to make the world
pronounce you with its lungs.

Your faith is wounded,
and you mistake the wound
for strength.

In a field of unbroken stems,
people scramble
to collect the falling facts;
with shoes plodding
over petals
and a trumpet-shaped corona,
and a smokestack voicing
the corrupted scream.

Tempting as it is,
to vanish like a prayer,
I remain here, for now,
in this Rust Belt town.

I am trudging beside
murky water,
spat up by a pipe
connected to waste
and ancient design;
it is now
a breeding ground
for blood-suckers.

A stranger lurks nearby,
I sense him behind me.
There is something
vaguely menacing about a whistle,
to even imagine
a grown man, walking along,
whistling out a tune,
I anticipate threat:
the joyous act
culturally undermined
by some cinematic sense
of foreboding.
But this stranger,
he keeps quiet
like the beautiful perennials.

Entering the neighborhood,
I likewise react
to the abrupt sound
of a sprinkler
like it's a hissing snake.

The mind was always wild,
it was never anything else.
The mind isn't pure order,
apart from nature;
the mind is part
of nature,
suspended in its own
murky water.

By the chance of gain,
or curious state of aggression,
we break boulders,
smashing pebbles
out of mass.
Mostly, we circumvent
obstacles or follow
beaten paths, abiding by
a map to find
that elusive destination
of true meaning:

some perpetual place
where no one lives for long.

It is strange also,
the way we feel a pull
toward other people, but this
way of thinking we sanitize
for our own health.

It is too mysterious
to wonder why
within mere seconds
of seeing a certain face,
the soul says,
"I am supposed to know you."
And when a person
defies this,
there is always
some unrest.

And we are forced
to wander.

~David Pring-Mill

Baggage from Rustling Pines

"Funny thing is, ghosts need an audience, an inner circle of admirers so to say, people who will vouch for them. Take them out of their comfort zone, and voila, they have an identity crisis." I twirled my fingers happily over my belly, and slid my toes out of the slippers to feel the cool sand in Daniel's backyard as he opened another beer for me.

We liked the new neighborhood already – a lot younger, but livelier, with the happy patter of baby feet and trike bells all day. Not the gloomy abode of sullen pensioners our previous one had. Nancy, my wife, was on the porch giggling with her new friends, helping add rosemary and garlic seasoning to the rib racks and briskets on the Weber water smoker. We men sat under the starlit sky drinking beer. This was a little welcome dinner organized for us by the neighbors.

"So, were the spooks for real," asked Danny, the banker guy staying across from us in the house with the blue roof with a corsage of houseleeks – brilliant yellow-green rosettes with amber colored tips.

"No one can say for sure, these are discarnate residuals, probably don't even know they've passed on. It all started when…" I waited for Brian to unpeel the oily wrapper on his Del Mundo cigar – he stayed to our left, in the house with the Ferrari in the drive.

"Started when?" he asked finally, puffing out thick clouds of rich cedar wood scented smoke.

"When the windows and doors on Mrs. Jankovic's house began banging all of a sudden one night."

"A wild animal?"

"One that can slide rusty bolts and turn door knobs? – Quite unlikely. A prankster maybe – but who would think of upsetting a lady with the husband out on combat duty in the Middle-East?"

"What was it then?"

"First she thought it was someone stalking her – it's so scary reading the papers these days. So she and her kids sprinkled talcum powder on the porch before turning in for the night. But the rattling and hullabaloo continued, with no footsteps on the powder on the floor.

Then she began to feel eyes upon her as she slept – burning ones – like red-hot coals. She was soon having chills and nightmares, and funny odors began to come from the house."

"Oh my," someone gasped as the ladies too joined us and sat around in a little agog circle.

"Yeah," I licked my mustache clean and waved the empty can. Someone quickly fetched another one. "So she calls over the local priest. He mumbo-jumbos some prayers, sprinkles holy water around the house and finds nothing. Telling her to find a better detergent and be more regular at Church, he promises to be back in a week."

"Did it help?"

"For a couple of days, yeah. And then it returned, much louder – she said she felt she was in the front row in a sledge metal rock concert."

"What'd she do then?"

"She called me in." I cleared my throat and puffed out my chest. "She called Nancy actually, and asked her for my help."

"Why you..." some doubter in the circle asked.

"Because I was a clerk with the Mayor's office, that's why." I searched the gathering for that cynical aspect but found only innocent curiosity. "And I happened to be the only man around."

"You see," Nancy quickly cut into the politely stifled titters, "there were only four houses on that row: Mrs. Jankovic's husband was away in Kuwait; Mrs. Wruck was a divorcee; Mrs. Algafari, a widow, was a Syrian refugee; and then ours. The houses across our road had been burnt down in a fire some twenty years ago."

"What did you do then, Max?"

"Well, I tipped the cops. Had them set up a vigil around her house for a couple of days – night visits ... surprise checks – just to make the lady feel comforted. Nancy told me how thankful Mrs. Jankovic was.

I thought things had been well taken care of, but when I reached home for lunch-break one afternoon, I found my own house locked up!"

"I'd heard some movement outside the house," Nancy chipped in. "So I thought it must be Max — he comes home most days for hot lunch you see — he hates carrying tiffin and microwaving it. Food tastes so damn rubbery he always says. So I come to the door and find I'm locked in — I think it's Max playing pranks on me — he does it all the time," she said, smiling coyly and patting down her bun of auburn hair.

"Yeah," I butted in, just in case Nancy got carried away. "We got only each other to fool around with. The kids are abroad — working with multinationals. I told her I would never scare her like that. Maybe it was a plumber, or an electrician, a Good Samaritan who might have rung the bell, and finding the door ajar — we let it stay open in the day mostly — closed it."

"But I got scared," Nancy added. "I'd just got over the phone call with Mrs. Jankovic — I knew how terrible it'd been for her. So I asked Max to check with people — just to make sure."

"I did check. A Good Samaritan is about as hard to come by as a square basketball. No one owned up to coming to my house — I think more out of embarrassment," I said.

"But I really got scared — in fact I began to check my door every now and then to make sure it wasn't bolted," Nancy added.

"It began to freak me out," I confessed. "Things really came to a head when somebody destroyed Mrs. Wruck's organic kitchen garden. She loved her veggies and made it a point to share her super foods with all of us.

We tried to tell her it must be some wild animal, but she wasn't convinced. She claimed animals would eat the plants, but in her case row upon row of kale, goji berries and kiwis had been systematically uprooted, as if the garden had been put to rest for winter."

"Poor woman!"

"Yeah, she was inconsolable; her plants were all she had for company — she sang to them and loved them like her own children.

Then one day, Nancy called me up when I was in a meeting with the school committee – she said it was urgent and I must rush home."

"What was it," asked Janice, the real estate agent who'd found us our new house at Bourbon, after we'd moved over from Rustling Pines.

"That was exactly my question when I found the ladies huddled in my house. Mrs. Algafari was beating her breast and wailing like a banshee – she'd found her clothes neatly packed into suitcases when she returned home after grocery shopping. She thought some evil man wanted to return her to her country!"

"Funny."

"Not so funny when you realize that she found the house locked exactly the way she'd left it – no tampering of the locks."

"Did you call in the cops," someone from the group asked – I didn't remember all the names as yet.

"That of course. But then we decided to do a little bit of introspection ourselves. Mrs. Jankovic became convinced that maleficent spirits haunted the place – she asked me to check the municipal records if any unnatural deaths had taken place in the area, or if any old burial grounds existed below our houses."

"Bad for property valuations," Janice said.

"True. I asked Herbert from Revenue to check – he came up with nothing. The houses across the road had been burnt after a forest fire, but they had been evacuated well in time. The property owners decided to move out rather than rebuild in the middle of the wilderness. And the terrain was too rocky to bury anything."

"Then?"

"The idea of a haunting was still far-fetched for me – a man of scientific temperament. Normally, we tend to give undue credit to paranormal phenomenon when none is deserved – I guess we just try to make sense of irrational things. I had another hunch though; with women there are always a lot of undercurrents – and when you have many of them who have never had to work a day in their lives bunched together, there are bound to be elves playing quietly under the surface."

There was light laughter and a clackety clack of tongues from our small group.

75

"That's not fair," somebody piped.

"Pardon me – I meant in a way that women are a complicated lot – they're deep, like still waters. So I asked this set if any inter-personal dynamics had changed of late… I mean if there was no other explanation, then it had to be a handiwork from within."

"You mean the girls were spiting each other for nothing better to do?"

"I dare not hold the worthy women of Rustling Pines, my loving wife included, in such poor esteem. No madam – I meant if anyone had moved in or out lately from our tiny, secluded community."

"And was there?"

I could see Nancy nodding, and about to speak up. I silenced her by holding up a hand. "Yes, apparently an old maid, a Filipino, who worked all the four houses, had recently been replaced. A good worker but had a mind of her own, and fond of talking back to the mistress of the house, which was not highly appreciated. The new maid was a Vietnamese, not so good, but a silent worker who'd replaced the Filipino."

"So what are you saying – the maid had something to do with it?"

"The Filipino had enjoyed absolute monopoly over the small colony. These Asian women always carry some old baggage – never see eye to eye – slit to slit with each other, I should perhaps say. Naturally some bitterness had to be there at losing lucrative employment."

"So it was the Filipino disturbing the peace!" There was a general sense of disappointment at the anti-climax of my story – some sighed and some made to rise, to add water and wood to the grill.

"That would be a rather simplistic explanation of the whole thing," I declared, sweeping my arm and bidding the gathering to remain seated. "We called the Filipino to our little council – naturally she acted very offended, and refused to own up to any mischief that had been plaguing us."

"Then you went back to the ghost?"

"Not so fast. Some of the ladies were unhappy with the new maid, and there'd been some murmurs about bringing the old one back; hints that were sometimes indiscreetly dropped within earshot of the new maid in the hope it would spur her to improve."

"So now it's the other maid?"

"She was also summoned, and she too went into denial. The general mood was in favor of holding the previous maid as the culprit. So to nab her, I suggested we keep a close watch on her movements."

"Did you catch her then?"

"Regrettably no. Meanwhile, Mrs. Jankovic nearly had a breakdown – her front gate had been torn down from its iron bolts, and there was shattered glass everywhere in her house. Enough was enough. I suggested we plant a CCTV near the entrance to the Filipino's servant quarters. You see, Mrs. Algafari out of kindness had allowed her to stay put till she found new work. Throwing out a network of cameras in all the houses was impractical, and would have become obvious. But a single camera could always be installed quietly."

"And the camera nailed her?"

The ribs seemed done with taking a luxurious bath in vapors. A delicious smoky smell wafted in from the grill, evoking strong atavistic memories. Daniel, our host, scratched the crusty grill with a fraying wire brush so that the black flecks sprayed on his baggy khaki shorts. "Smoke," he declared, "is the sixth taste of food: after salty, sweet, sour, bitter and umami."

He picked up a slab with tongs and bounced it slightly till it bowed to the point of breaking. "It's done, here, try," he said. I could pull the ribs clean off the bones with my teeth. Daniel reached for another slab, but his wife, Debbie, slapped away his hand with an oven mitt. "Leave something for the guests." She laughed, her pearly teeth catching the glint of fair moonlight. She put sauce on the meat and let it sizzle some. "Go on, finish the story, I'll hear it from Daniel tonight," she said. We grabbed some more beers from the icebox and passed them around in the group.

"Where was I," I asked when people had clicked open the cans. Some ladies got up to help Debbie with the servings.

"You put up a camera..."

"Oh yes. Nothing changed though. The Syrian woman receives a call from the train station one day, that two of her suitcases, with nameplates, packed, were found by the Station Master with an outbound ticket pasted on! She was terror-stricken and refused to step out of her house.

Mrs. Wruck found slabs of wild boar meat, still bloodied, in her fridge. A sworn vegetarian – it was like blasphemy to her. And let me tell you – it's not easy to kill wild boar."

"And what about you Nancy…nothing went on in your house," asked Janice.

"Well," Nancy replied, " I found the new maid's three-month old baby in my living room one morning – how it got there, nobody knows. The maid was hysterical, and I was too. I screamed at Max to get me out of that place."

"I felt I had a responsibility to make the women feel secure." I added. " I felt they were on my watch. And I had failed. The cops assembled everyone in my house and checked the footage on the CCTV. Alas, the Filipino maid had never stirred from her quarters – she was laid low with the chills and malaise. They called in the new maid then – who would believe a woman would dump her own baby in someone's house just to spite the competition?

But after sustained interrogation – the cops have their methods; they managed to extract a confession from the woman that she'd *probably* forgotten the child after working our house! She still denied any wrongdoings in the other houses though."

"What did you do then?"

"Obviously it was a very convenient explanation, too feeble a defense even to imagine. She was lying; she was sacked, expunged from the neighborhood post haste."

"Thank God! Surely it was all calm thereafter…why did everyone leave then, Max?"

"True, it was calm—the rattlings ceased. Mrs. Wruck's green leafy salads topped with juicy red tomatoes flourished again. No one made any more moves to evacuate the Syrian. Nancy, my darling here," I said, ruffling her mop of unruly hair, "was no longer immured within four walls of the house against her wishes."

"What women will not do to have their way?" Daniel chuckled, poking Brian in the ribs with a rib licked clean.

"Nothing, I think," I replied. "A month later, Herbert – you remember him from the Revenue records – called. He said one servant family was still sleeping in when the forest fires started. They couldn't make their escape – they fell unconscious with the CO_2 fumes. The couple perished in the flames."

"But you said he'd checked the records – and there had been no deaths recorded?"

"Exactly what I asked him. He said they had a daughter with a domicile at Minnesota. She applied for the death certificates in that state because of some insurance issues, and had the municipal records transferred there. He happened to notice it only when the blanks were thrown up during an audit when town archives were being transcribed into automated records. He remembered I'd been making inquiries and how anxious Nancy had been. Nice of him to have told us."

"Are we back to ghosts now," Debbie asked, and suddenly shivered. Daniel wrapped her in close embrace.

"Utter baloney, I assure you, friends. I told Herbert to rest easy because we'd found peace after the deportation of the new maid – the matter had been settled."

"That's a relief to know."

"Mrs. Jankovic though, on learning of the new development, managed to convince the others to fence the plot and give some kind of a decent burial service to the departed souls – just in case."

"What about the property valuations?" Janice pointed out.

"Smart people think alike," I replied. She made a small bow and spread her arms in acknowledgment.

"That's what I told the other folks. You see; we were done with that place. My retirement was coming up in a few months, and the others seemed fed up too. Mrs. Jankovic was the least affected because she would have moved out once her husband returned from his tour of duty. Mrs. Wruck found only rock below the topsoil and was finding it harder to rejuvenate her garden with each passing season. Mrs. Algafari was the hardest to convince. But I knew once singled out, she too would go along with the others."

"Still you managed to sell the property?"

"I told the others if we fenced off the land or did anything emotional, it would sink the market rates. And I won't be lying if I told you that this developer had been hounding me on the quiet to have the complete plot vacated so that he could take it over. He wanted to build warehouses and a solar power plant on the property."

"Was there an incentive involved?"

I cleared my throat. "Let us say there was good in it for everybody – in proportion to the efforts involved. With the power transformers toasting overhead – I assured the others the dear departed souls, if there were any, would get a lifelong last rites service – a proper *cremation* free on the house. And that was it – we kept quiet, we all sold off to this developer, and moved to different places – listening to the jingle of spare change in our pockets. We made a great deal." Looking around the tony locale, where I now belonged, I smacked my lips in satisfaction.

"Not bad – you saved the day for the others – old women by themselves wouldn't have been able to salvage such a good value from a bad deal," said the banker.

I chuckled and patted Danny warmly on his back, "I felt like Moses who'd led his people across the sea."

With that we rose. The night was still, the wind had died, and the stars had dimmed in the deepening twilight. Suddenly the quietness was disturbed with rising, anxious voices. I stepped over to the small circle gathered around Debbie who was trying to wrench open the porch door so that she could fetch cutlery from the kitchen.

"I swear I left this door open," she was repeating hysterically. Others peered through the window into the house. "Damn! The house is locked from inside!"

Slowly the people turned towards me. The look of admiration and envy of a few moments ago seemed to have been swept aside by plain loathing, fear.

Toast the ghost, will you, smartass Max? Ghosts need people to vouch for them – didn't you say so yourself? You've hauled in unwanted baggage from Rustling Pines and heaped it upon us – their seething eyes seemed to crackle and spit.

I wondered if someone would be ready to build an expensive shopping arcade here. This land was too precious to be wasted on street parks and urban farmhouses.

~Nidhi Singh

Country Funeral

down the rambling
path they led us to the open
mouth of earth

where I would lay to rest
someone I never met
lifting a cask gently.

~*Alan Inman*

Soft Grass Murmur

the animal
hiding on its haunches
a few yards away

gives us no warning
before its charge
interrupting our lakeside
meal and rest.

~Alan Inman

Redemption

"So thanks again for letting me stay here the night." John said.

"Yes, you're not the first one to get lost. I am known as Fishwick around these parts." The old man replied, cleaning his glasses with a dirty looking cloth. "What happened to your car?" the man asked, pointing at the broken headlights.

"Animals." He replied in a nervous manner.

John took the rucksack off his shoulders, exhausted. Well it wasn't a fancy room, but it would do him for now. The house creaked as the rain fell heavy on the pavement and John lit a cigarette. He looked at his watch, a few more hours until dawn. His mind kept going over what happened. He was an obliging, hardworking man, but something that morning just went wrong. Instead of heading out to work as normal, he packed a bag, just in case. He got to the car park at work, hesitated for a few minutes, and then drove out. No destination in mind.

After driving in a daze, he found himself in the woods. That's when, in a split second, everything changed. He was in the wrong place at the wrong time some might say. He never saw the man coming. This young man ran across the road, out of nowhere, and the car struck him instantly. He did not move, laid there on the ground barely breathing...*He'll be dead in minutes*. John did not wait to find out, and he just left him there.

How would he explain what had happened? He panicked. There would be questions. Pointing fingers. Press coverage. He had done everything right for such a long time. Now everything felt wrong to him.

He put his cigarette out and laid on his back, eyes shut. At first he thought that his mind was playing tricks on him. But there was a continuous whistling sound coming from one of the corners. He got up to get closer to it, and there it was behind the wall, getting stronger and stronger.

"Anyone there?" John asked.

Nothing.

I am going mental. Perhaps it was all that chaos earlier?

"Sin," it whispered.

"Look, this is not funny. Who is there?"

The creaking noise started again, and the wall started to shake and break in places. John placed the palm of his right hand against it and felt the vibrations opening small cracks on the wall, and then a dripping sound started. Drop. Drop. Drop.

In the dim light John touched the wet floor and followed the traces, which were filling the cracks on the wall. In bloody red ink it spelled "S I N".

"What the hell?" John cried in a muted scream, his voice closed in on itself.

A loud knock on his door made him jump. The door opened without waiting for a reply. An old man stood in the doorway.

"What have you done son?" The old man asked, his expression somber and sad.

"Nothing, I was just lying down and…" John never finished the sentence as the old man interjected.

"No, I meant what have you done? What crime?" He voiced accusingly.

John's face became expressionless. The sigh of relief had been replaced by a haunting feeling of desperation.

"I…. I didn't. It was an accident. " He replied.

"You must have done something son, otherwise you wouldn't be here." The old man muttered.

John said nothing.

"I am the Keeper, the guardian of this house. It claims all sinners." Fishwick said breaking the silence. "Repent or the house will claim you!"

John shook his head, nothing but nonsense he thought. *He couldn't possibly know. No one could.* Fishwick was probably some lonely old lunatic toying with him. *This was just a desolate worn out place at the end of the world.*

"I will say it again, son. Repent or---"

"If you think I'm scared of you, you've got another thing coming." John menaced.

"Son, there isn't much time." The old man said in a tone of sorrow. His warning was followed shortly by a loud roar from the walls. Mr. Fishwick stepped back and stared at the young man before him. "Too late," he whispered.

"What's too late? Wait right there." John said leaning against the wall as the ground beneath him started to shake.

"Stop this, old man!"

"I am afraid this is not my doing."

"Help me old man! Please!"

Fishwick lowered his eyes, retreating back to the front porch.

"Help. I have done nothing wrong. Shit... I did not mean to leave him to die. Please, I am sorry! Help!"

John's cries quickly disappeared as the floor opened up, swallowing his body. The house growled one last time, and then everything fell into darkness and silence. Fishwick closed the door behind him. Not this time. Not yet. He whispered, a tear rolling down his cheek. Suddenly the sound of an engine stalling outside the house prompted him to the window. Two men were pushing a car up the drive. It had run out of gas.

"Look man. It's a guesthouse. Let's park up here." A redhead boy said, pointing to the old sign, which hung by the streetlight, rocking back and forth in the evening breeze. It read, "Redemption".

Fishwick went to the door. "It will be 45 for the night. Two of you?"

"Yes, man, thanks. We ran out of gas. Our cell phones have no reception?"

"No reception around these parts, I'm afraid. Mr.?"

"Well we can use your phone and call for assistance."

"No phone lines at all, I'm afraid." Fishwick said.

"Really?" the man sounded surprised. "Well, I am Will and this is Matt."

"And what have you too been up to?"

"Camping." Matt, the dark haired one, replied.

Will interjected, "Well we were going to, but with the weather you see. We have come from the city."

The old man looked at them for a moment.

"Well, you are a long way from home. Here is your key."

"Hey man, we meant to ask. Was that an earthquake earlier?"

"I didn't feel anything," Fishwick answered. *How long will it take this time?*

"Has it been busy old man?" Matt asked maliciously.

"Yes it has been a very busy season as a matter of fact." Fishwich replied. He didn't like these two.

"How long have you worked here?" Will asked, looking around the lobby.

"Too long. Care to take my place?"

"Nah, no thanks." Will shook his head.

The men had barely settled into their room when the house came to life.

Here we go again. Fishwick pressed the bedroom door open. "Repent, or the house will kill you."

"Are you crazy?" Will shouted. "Get out man."

"I suggest you confess your sins. You may have a chance of surviving."

A loud noise started rattling the windows and mirrors in the room. "What have you done?" Fishwick asked again.

Matt was scared and broke down first, "Listen man. Ok maybe you saw. We went camping with our buddy Tommy. We were just playing pranks on him, ok. We got drunk, we didn't mean to fire the gun."

"Shut up Matt." Will instructed.

"He's gonna kill us Will."

"No he won't. Look at him."

The house shook violently once again and the growling began.

"Ok Mister, listen. Will fired the gun and shot Tommy in the leg. It was an accident. Nothing more."

"And then what?" Fishwick asked.

"Enough." Shouted Will.

But Matt didn't stop. "We think Tommy panicked. He just ran towards the road. Next thing we know we heard a bang. We ran to him but he was on the ground in the middle of the road. I think he was hit by a car."

"Was he dead?" Fishwick asked.

"No. He wasn't." Matt said crying. "He was like a wounded animal. We got scared you see. That no one would believe us. Jail for life for sure."

"So what did you do next?"

"Nothing. Matt is making all this stuff up. Shut up you fool." Will shouted.

"Or what Will?" Matt asked. "We finished him off. That's what we did." He carried on sobbing. "I am so sorry. I am so sorry. We didn't mean to kill." He kept repeating.

The house fell silent. All three men froze. Large writings on the wall read "REPENT". *Could this be it?* Fishwick stood back and grabbed Matt. His heart was pounding. The room split into to two. Will was thrown onto the floor and quickly sunk and disappeared amongst the screams.

And as soon as it had started it all ended. Matt could not move or say a word.

"I can't tell you how long I have been waiting for you." Fishwick said.

"What?" Matt managed to utter.

"You have done it. You confessed your sins. The house let you live and now this is your act of contrition." He sighed. "Your friend however didn't. And that's what happens."

"Wait. What now? Where are you going?" Matt asked.

"You are the new Innkeeper, Matt. It's all yours." Fishwick muttered.

~*Janete Cabral-Jackson*

The Fall of King Marty

The punch almost sends Isaac's head all the way around his body, kind of like those cartoons he used to watch when he was younger. He is suddenly spinning, gravity seizing control of his body and pulling all 72 pounds of his frail and skinny frame to the concrete below. He lands with a smack, his palms scraping against the sidewalk. Blood and spittle dangle loosely from his face, seeping together in a steady stream from where the impact had occurred.

Isaac is happy to land face down, happy to not have to look up at the mob of his peers that have gathered around him. A cacophony of laughs and chants reverberate through his eardrums. He recognizes some of the voices, kids who would never utter the slightest indecency towards him in any other circumstance. Through the raucous, he can make out the thunderous voice of Marty Ortiz, it seems to be feeding off the crowd.

"Get up! C'mon!" he roars.

But Isaac can't move. He simply lays there—his overstuffed backpack pushed up at his head. He tastes blood in his mouth. It collides with the residue of his mother's turkey sandwich from earlier.

"Get up!" Marty repeats. "Get up!"

Isaac's double vision begins to align once more. He considers getting up and throwing a punch, but refrains.

"You're really just going to sit there?"

Isaac says nothing.

"You're no fun."

WHACK! A kick goes straight to his stomach. The impact causes him to curl up into a ball, grabbing for his knees as the pain spiders its way across his body. A moment later, the crowd is dispersing. He glances up at Marty as he walks away, striding triumphantly as if he'd just won a game of dodge ball.

The 7th grader has enormous arms, his fingertips reach all the way down to his knees when he walks. His back is arched as if his shoulders are hard to carry. Isaac thinks that it is entirely plausible that one of his grandparents is a grizzly bear.

Once the last of Marty's goons has cleared, Isaac pushes himself up from the ground. He wonders if the teachers will catch wind of the fight. He wonders if they'll care. After last time, Marty learned his lesson about picking fights *during* school hours. He now has a strict thirty-minute post dismissal policy.

"My god you're a mess!" cries Isaac's mother. She almost drops her plate of organic kosher lasagna when he enters the room. Now, she's got her son up on the kitchen table, dabbing his nose with wet paper towels to remove the dried blood.

"Is it broken?"

"I don't think so."

"Look at me."

She maneuvers Isaac's head to the left and then right. She touches each side gently.

"Does that hurt?"

"A little."

"Who keeps doing this to you?"

"Why'd you put onions on my turkey sandwich?"

"Isaac, answer my question."

Her scrubbing gets more intense as she realizes Isaac is not in pain.

"Different kids," says Isaac. The thought of his mother calling Marty's household is his worst nightmare. "I'm small, an easy target."

"You're not small."

"To them I am."

Isaac's mom pulls his head into her chest.

"Why'd you put onions on my turkey sandwich?"

"You told me you like them now."

"They taste like crap."

"Watch your mouth!" she says, while resuming repairs.

~~~OOO~~~

Later that night, Juan moves Isaac's desk chair underneath his doorknob, sealing away all figures of authority. Isaac slips into a pair of boxing gloves. They are too big on his hands. In his head, he looks like a lobster. Juan opens his backpack and pulls out two hitting mitts. He puts them on. Lobster best friends.

"Right!" Juan calls.

Isaac throws his right fist.

"Right! Left! Right! Right!"

Isaac throws the punches as best he can but Juan is significantly taller. Juan throws his right mitt. Isaac dodges. He throws his left, catches Isaac off guard. Flakes of dried blood bounce onto the leather.

"Careful!" shouts Juan. "Don't bleed on my brother's gloves."

"Is this training even working?" asks Isaac.

"Of course it is! You're much stronger than when we started. Left! Left! Right!"

"But I'm not gonna have these gloves when I fight Marty again."

"Doesn't matter, my brother says boxing is about form."

Isaac begins to sweat. The salt stings the cut underneath his nose.

"Guard the face," says Juan. "Always guard the face."

"I can't guard the face, I have to reach all the way up! He's big—"

"But you're fast. My brother says he'd rather be fast than big any day."

Isaac pauses momentarily. He topples over on his knees, panting and out of breath.

"I'm scared," Isaac admits in between wheezes.

Juan looks over at his best friend, studies his fragile frame. Juan is just as gawky and thin, but at least he has height on his side.

"Don't be afraid. He'll never see us coming. We're going to take down King Marty once and for all. Got it?"

Isaac nods, his hands still pressed to his knees — They both know he hasn't got it.

The next day Isaac stands at his locker. He will soon be in 6th grade, the supposed top of the elementary school food chain. He's waited his whole life to be at the top, but right now it doesn't seem like it matters. There will always be a bigger fish. Or in his case, a grizzly bear.

He rearranges his textbooks so that they are ordered alphabetically. He doesn't remember when he started doing it, nor does he know why. Isaac feels a sense of safety by his locker, a sense of control. As a younger kid, Isaac was obsessed with hideouts and secret lairs. He would build forts out of blankets and chairs in his room. He would draw lavish maps of his house, complete with their own secret passages and hidden tunnels. His locker, a private space accessed only by the combination in his brain, appeals to that same sense of control.

"Hey jerk-face!"

And all control is relinquished. The call sends a shiver down Isaac's spine, he can feel his fingers begin to tremble. He stares into the metal of his locker, trying to ignore the colossal mass moving into peripheral. A shove to his left shoulder wheels him around to catch a glimpse of the oncoming predator.

"Mommy clean you up alright?" Marty asks.

Three of his goons stand right behind him. They laugh on cue, almost as if the moment has been rehearsed. Marty is dressed in an oversized t-shirt. He wears a bandana across his forehead. He catches a glimpse of puffy swelling beneath Isaac's nose.

"Doesn't look too bad," Marty continues. "You should consider yourself lucky."

"Please leave me alone, Marty," Isaac whispers.

"Oh, you *can* speak. I was beginning to worry."

"Kick his ass again!" shouts a goon.

"Not during school hours, you know my policy."

He turns back towards his victim.

"Heal up fast," Marty says. "I'm itching for round two."

He strides off down the hallway. Isaac begins to turn towards his locker.

"Jerk-face," he mutters under his breath.

He's not even conscious of it coming out, a verbal reflex spit up like a cough.

"What did you call me?"

Marty has stopped in his tracks and now Isaac's stomach is twisting itself into a pretzel. He wants to throw up, he wants to run, but his feet ground themselves to the floor. In an instant, Marty has him pinned him against the lockers, screws rattling behind the aluminum exterior. Isaac turns his head, dejecting this intrusion into his personal space. He squirms behind the statue-like arms of his captor.

"Tomorrow, 3 pm," growls Marty, his putrid breath seeping into Isaac's pores. "I'll beat you so bad mommy won't even recognize you."

He releases his grip and this time Isaac topples over, his back scrapping against the knobs of the lockers below. Isaac remains there for a moment before pulling himself to his feet. He continues to alphabetize his textbooks.

Juan finds Isaac in the cafeteria, eating alone and pulling onions off a turkey sandwich. Juan slams his hands onto the table, his face lit up with excitement.

"I need to talk to you," he almost shouts.

Isaac follows his best friend out onto the schoolyard, the early afternoon sun baking the painted asphalt around them.

They make their way to a table where Becca Munson and Rachel Lee are selling Girl Scout cookies. They sit there, roasting in their green uniforms, container of cash to their right with brochures on their left. Behind them, a teacher halfheartedly patrols two enormous boxes of Girl Scout cookies.

"Becca!" Juan shouts as he approaches the table. "Becca, I need you to tell Isaac what you told me earlier."

Becca glances up at the two. She shrugs her shoulders playing dumb.

"I'm not sure what I told you, Juan."

"You know exactly what you told me."

"Then why can't *you* just tell him?"

"I need him to hear it from the source."

"You'll have to buy a box — Rah-Rah Raisins."

Juan's face drops in disgust.

"Raisins? You want me to buy *raisin* cookies? Are you out of your mind?"

"No one will buy them. We have to reach our goal."

Isaac fishes around for a crumbled $5 bill in his pocket. He pulls it out and hands it to Becca.

"Rah Rah Raisins, Ms. Fisher," Rachel calls back.

The teacher pulls out a box of cookies and tosses it onto the table, her eyes barely lifting from her cell phone screen. Isaac begins to wonder who is in charge of who.

"Alright," Becca begins. "You never heard this from me, got it?"

Isaac nods.

"Marty Ortiz still sleeps with stuffed animals."

Isaac's eyes widen, the shouts and screams of the schoolyard begin to fade away. He takes a step closer to the table, his brain beginning to sputter through an array of hypotheticals.

"Go on," is all he says.

"Well, Allie Keating and her mom were selling cookies on Marty's block. If she sells all her cookies in three different districts she gets her community badge —"

"The stuffed animals, Becca," Juan interrupts.

"Right, well Allie Keating's mom and Marty Ortiz's mom have been friends since Mommy and Me, so Marty's Mom invited them in for a house tour. When they got to Marty's room, his bed was COVERED in stuffed animals. Allie asked Marty's Mom if they were all his and she said yes and that he has names for all of them. His favorite is a stuffed bunny rabbit known as Mr. Toothy that Allie's Mom bought for Marty when he was only four."

A smile flashes across his face, the biggest he's worn in weeks. He's a lawyer that's found his case, a stockbroker primed to cash in on a big tip. His fingertips begin to pulse with the prospect of opportunity.

"Thanks Becca," he says coolly.

Isaac grabs his box of raisin cookies and begins to make his way back across the yard. Juan tails him emphatically.

"What do you think?" Juan shouts.

"Marty wants to fight me again tomorrow. Can you imagine the look on his face when I pull Mr. Toothy out of my bag? He's going to be the laughing stock of the 7th grade."

"Wait, wait, wait. So that means you want to—"

"—Exactly Juan," he says gleefully. "We're going to kidnap Mr. Toothy."

After school, they stand across the street from Marty's house, a rectangular two-story structure. "Alright," Isaac begins, "we're not going to have a lot of time."

He pulls out a homemade map of Marty's house, a crude draft of lines and arrows complete with secret passageways and hidden vaults.

"If my calculations are correct, then Marty's lair sits at the top left corner—"

"—his room?"

"Whatever. It would be that window right over there." He said, gesturing to a window sitting right above a cluster of thick green bushes.

"I can get out but I can't get in. So you'll be the distraction while I sneak in through the front. Then you'll wait on the side of the house where I'll hop out via that window."

"What if Marty comes home?"

"He won't. He's got a 2:45 appointment to beat up Dennis Leftkowtiz."

"Got it."

The two make their way to the front door where Juan stands stupidly. Isaac hides behind a nearby bush. Juan knocks. The door is opened by a stern looking woman who is ungodly tall. She wears workout clothes, tight black spandex, and a bright green tank top. To Isaac's dismay, she looks nothing like a grizzly bear. He watches as Juan begins to fidget in place, the box of Girl Scout cookies by his side.

"Hello," he stammers. "Would you like to buy some Girl Scout cookies?"

He holds out the box of Rah-Rah Raisin Cookies.

Marty's Mom stares back at him, entirely dumbfounded.

"You don't look like a Girl Scout," she replies.

"I'm selling them for my sister."

Marty's Mom still looks skeptical.

"She's very busy but needs to sell out in three districts to get her community badge," he adds.

"I see," she says, thinking to herself. "How much?"

"$5."

"How do I know you're not just pocketing the money?" asks Marty's Mom.

Juan says nothing. He looks stumped. Finally Marty's Mom lets out a laugh.

"I'll get my wallet."

She turns to head inside. Juan shoots Isaac a thumbs up and suddenly Isaac is booking it for the door, the swaying of his backpack throwing him off balance. He slips into the house unnoticed.

Isaac's first thought is that Marty's home seems just like his, family photos and quirky artwork strung about. He finds himself in an entry hallway. He can hear Marty's Mom fumbling around in the kitchen at the other end. Isaac turns and books it up the staircase on his left. He realizes his map is already wrong.

The first room that Isaac enters is clearly the master bedroom, much too large for Marty and not nearly evil enough. He continues down until he finds the room in the corner, which he had guessed to be that of his nemesis. He pushes open the door to reveal a teenager's bedroom. Adolescent symbols coat the walls, everything from car posters to sports memorabilia. The room is pristine, clearly having just been made. And again, Isaac is struck with the unnerving revelation that *he* could just as easily live in this particular secret hideout.

Remembering his objective, he scans the room from left to right. A sense of horror overwhelms his body, the lump in his throat growing thicker by the second. There are no stuffed animals. Nothing. Not a single embarrassing item in plain view.

Isaac sifts through his options. He knows he doesn't have too much time. There has to be something in this room that he could use. Maybe the stuffed animals were hidden by his mother or a maid. He gets to his knees and looks under the bed. Nothing. He opens the closet and peers behind a rack of shirts. Nothing. He checks the trunk by Marty's bed. Nothing. Isaac can hear the door shut downstairs. He's officially locked in.

Accepting his failure, Isaac heads to the window and begins to unlatch it. Suddenly, he notices a big drawer to the right of Marty's desk. He shuffles over and pulls it open to reveal a stack of comic books and old school assignments. The drawer is stuffed to the brim, papers overflowing from each side. Isaac begins to frantically pull them out. No stuffed animals. No Mr. Toothy. He keeps digging and digging and then he stops. At the bottom of the drawer is a thick stack of magazines — with men — lots of them. They're all naked, kissing and touching each other. They're brightly colored. The covers feature strange words in weird fonts.

Isaac pauses. He glances around the room, deep in thought, his brain churning to make sense what he's found. Then — he reaches for the pile and slips the stack of magazines into his backpack. He returns the rest of the drawer's contents and heads for the window.

Isaac plops into the shrubbery below from the second story, his backpack absorbs the majority of the impact. Twigs and branches snap around him to accommodate his landing. He rolls out to the right side of the house, skin scraped and with leaves in his hair. Juan is there to greet him.

"Did you get it?" Juan asks. "Did you get Mr. Toothy?"

"No but I did—"

Isaac stops himself. He doesn't know why. For some reason doesn't want to tell Juan what he's found.

"Allie Keating is a liar," he says instead.

At 2:45 the next afternoon, Isaac stands at his locker. The halls are empty, classrooms deserted. He knows what waits for him outside. He can see the mass of bodies beginning to congregate at the school's entrance. He reaches into his locker and pulls out a map of the premises, reassesses his exit routes. He imagines being able to will the secret passages he's drawn into reality.

At 2:59 Isaac heads for the exit, a prisoner marching to his execution. He pushes himself through the front doors and attempts to sidestep the group of boys without being noticed. He hits the base of the steps and immediately starts in the direction of his house.

"Hey, jerk-face, where are you going so fast?!" shouts Marty playfully. He stands in front of a group of older boys, skateboard tucked underneath his arm. The goons take all shapes and sizes — they watch their leader subserviently.

"I'm going home, Marty," Isaac replies stiffly, shocked by his own confidence.

"That's bull," Marty scoffs. "We have an appointment."

"I'd like to reschedule."

Marty emerges from the crowd and grabs Isaac by the strap of his backpack. He pulls him left and right, a puppeteer with masterful control. Finally, he lets go, the momentum change causes Isaac to fall and hit the lawn.

"No rescheduling," Marty continues, a big smile across his face. "I was going to leave you alone for a while. I almost felt bad for bashing your nose in. But you had to be a smart ass yesterday."

Isaac pulls himself to his knees, coughing loudly. His hands are covered in soot and soil. The grizzly bear approaches and squats next to his wounded prey.

"Don't talk back to your elders, Isaac," Marty whispers. "It's not nice."

He then stands up and heads back towards his goons, rolling up the sleeves of his pleather jacket and cracking his meaty knuckles. Isaac recognizes his opportunity. He gets to his feet, unzips the backpack and pulls out the stack of magazines he found earlier. He holds them high above his head, his hand trembling.

"Recognize these, Marty?" Isaac squeaks. "I thought you may want them back."

And the smile drips off Marty's face. His eyes widen, vulnerable and cracked. His body tenses up, he seems to sink into the concrete ever so slightly. The crowd of boys watch on, confused both by Isaac's defiance as well as his method of defying.

And then — Marty snaps back, reverts to beast. His shoulders round once more, the lines begin to crease in his forehead. And like a firework, he explodes off the pavement, his arms wrapping around Isaac's frame and sending him to the ground with a crack. Isaac's neck snaps back against the grass as Marty drives his knee into his chest. Marty throws a clean punch squarely into Isaac's jaw.

"You piece of shit!" he shouts. "You little piece of shit!"

And he's whacking Isaac with everything he has, pulverizing him into the grass. Marty's gone mad, rage sweeping through his body. The crowd is not laughing, they gaze on in horror, astonished by their king's hysterics. Marty doesn't fight like a predator or a bully or a king. He fights like a crazed dog, driven not by a sense of superiority but survival.

When Isaac comes to, he can barely see the tree branches above him through his swollen eyes. All he can taste is blood and dirt. His chest feels like it's about to cave in. One of Marty's goons crouches above him.

"Isaac," the goon calls, his voice sounds miles away. "Can you stand up? We need to get you to the nurse."

Isaac finds the strength to turn his head towards the boy next to him. He finds that the crowd has dispersed. Marty is gone. A few kids sit around him, watching intently for signs of life.

"I want to go home," Isaac coughs. "Please, I want to go home."

The next week, Isaac's Mom pulls him out of school. She spends hours researching private institutions, reworks the family finances to try and come up with options.

Meanwhile, upstairs, Juan finds that Isaac has no interest in practicing boxing. His best friend has two black eyes, a busted lip, and abrasions on his forehead and cheek.

"C'mon! Don't get discouraged," Juan says. "My brother says that knockouts are a part of boxing. Next time, we're going to get him good."

"I don't think so, Juan," Isaac replies. "I don't want to fight anyone ever again."

"What are you talking about? He pulverized you. We need to get revenge."

Isaac studies himself in the mirror, examines his battered face. Why doesn't he feel like he lost the fight? There is a knock on his door.

"Isaac!" his mother calls from behind it. "There is someone at the door for you."

Isaac and Juan both race to the window and glare out at the street below. There, on the sidewalk, stands Marty. Except he doesn't look like Marty. He wears a hoodie and gym shorts. His head hangs low and his posture is extra slouched.

"Oh no," Juan whispers. "What does he want?"

"I'm not sure," replies Isaac.

"You want me to go down there with you?"

"No."

"Thank God."

Isaac makes his way down the stairs and towards the front door. He is not afraid. He doesn't know why, but he is not afraid.

He crosses the doorframe and out onto the ledge. Marty is crying hysterically, with puffy eyes and bright red cheeks. He runs the sleeve of his sweater across a snotty nose, deep pulsing sobs shaking his entire body. Isaac simply stares. He remains perfectly still, afraid to make any sudden movements.

"Can I have my magazines back?" Marty whimpers.

The two stare silently at each other for a few minutes. And suddenly Isaac understands—he reads Marty like a map, secret passages and all.

He disappears inside for a moment before returning with Marty's magazines. He silently hands them over. Marty takes the stack and holds it to his chest like a prized book. His crying intensifies. Then he turns and begins to walk away, dragging his legs over the concrete like they are too heavy to lift.

Isaac returns to his room to find Juan already on his feet. He's watched the whole interaction from the window.

"What did he want?!" Juan shouts.

"He wanted to say 'sorry,'" he replies.

"That's not very king-like."

"No," Isaac says, thinking to himself, "I don't think it is."

~Daniel Tobin

We Will Never Forget You

Katie faints, falls down the steps, and breaks her wrist. In the news reports, her injury is counted among the others caused by the tragedy at the high school that day.

The night before, she is rattled out of her sleep, over and over, into cold sheets reeking of sweat. Too nervous to eat breakfast that morning, she walks to school in a low-blood sugar daze. It is October, and the sun has not yet burned off the hazy grey filter that veils the beige and white homes and auburn-leafed trees that line the road.

Today she is late, and the east entrance is deserted. Halfway up the steps, she collapses backwards. When she opens her eyes, she sees the overcast sky. The lockdown alert booms in her ears. She tries to push herself up until she feels a shooting pain chase up her left arm.

A squad of emergency medical technicians bursts through the school's door, looking for victims. They assume Katie is one of them. They assess her pulse and breathing, and roll her body over, looking for a bullet wound.

The EMTs lift her onto a stretcher and carry her into an ambulance. She can't see out any windows but can feel the ambulance accelerating. She can hear the siren and a ceiling vent blows hot, dry air into her face.

"Can you hear me?" an EMT asks.

"My wrist. It hurts."

"Can you wiggle your fingers for me? What do you remember?"

"I think I fell."

The tech begins to splint her wrists and then applies an ice pack. "Huh. You aren't bleeding and we couldn't find any entry points. We're taking you in for an assessment anyway."

Katie can feel a pulse inside her swollen wrist pressing against the splint, and the tech gives her a pill for the pain. But that pain is pushed aside by a calm euphoria.

She will not have to give the speech today. The speech that made her heart stop when she saw it on the syllabus at the beginning of the semester. The speech she refused to give twice already. Mr. Davenport insisted that she would get no better than a "D" in his communications class if she ditched school on the day she was scheduled to speak. "D" for damned, her chances at becoming valedictorian and fulfilling the expectations of her family and herself. She needed an "A" in what was an easy class, apart from a two-minute speech on American history.

Lost in the ambulance's lunging lane changes and awash in the catharsis of her unexpected respite, she smiles.

"You having trouble breathing? I'm going to give you some oxygen, okay? Hold still." The tech puts a non-rebreather mask over Katie's nose and mouth and slips a strap behind her head. "Better?" he asks.

Katie feels better than she has in days. When they arrive at the hospital, the EMT who tied the splint consults with a triage nurse. "Just a sprained wrist, best I can tell."

She is wheeled to a spot in a hallway, and another nurse brings her a cup of water and blanket. She can hear a television nearby.

We interrupt the Price is Right with some unfortunate news. An armed individual opened fire at Andrews High School this morning. We are now aware of at least eight fatalities and twenty-five others who were injured and are being treated at hospitals throughout the metro region. Among the fatalities is the alleged shooter who we are told turned the gun on himself when cornered by police.

Katie sits up and takes a sip from her cup as a gurney ushered by two men and two women in white coats approaches. One of them is holding up a bag of fluid. They are running and shouting at each other. As they race by, Katie sees a face that she recognizes, covered in blood.

Katie first met Allie in kindergarten. They were "cubby buddies," sharing one of the wooden supply boxes that lined the open classroom's wall. In middle school, they were among a clique of girls who had sleepovers and traded gossip and future plans of fame, wealth, and celebrity marriages.

In high school, differing schedules and diverging interests separated them. Allie was on the cheer squad and ran cross-country, while Katie was absorbed by college-prep and advanced placement classes. They still found occasions to get together, and the two of them would laugh over the desperate, clichéd poems that boys would slip into their lockers.

Katie watches Allie's gurney disappear around the corner.

The next day, the news reports confirm the names of the dead. Allie is on the list, along with two other girls from their old clique. Three days later, the community holds a memorial service. Katie attends with her parents. She hasn't eaten anything since the night before the shooting and passes out again.

Two weeks later, classes resume at an unused elementary school with several dozen additional classrooms set up in trailers. Surviving members of the girls' and boys' cross country teams pledge to win the state championship for their fallen teammates. Some students form a club to petition the state to ban firearms. Other students form a club to advocate for arming teachers.

The students most affected by the shooting are assigned grief counselors by the school district. At her first and only session, Katie says nothing, shrugging and staring at the floor when the counselor asks how she feels.

In each classroom, the homeroom students make a memorial for their dead peers. In the mornings, a loud, universal cheer erupts throughout the school as the principal announces over the PA system the names of the injured students who are returning to regular attendance that day.

Katie's is failing all of her classes. Her parents hire a tutor and a psychotherapist. The psychiatrist prescribes pills Katie refuses to take. Her mother, noticing how poorly Katie's clothes are fitting, makes her stand on a scale. Eight-eight pounds. Katie is five-foot six. Her mother schedules an appointment with a nutritionist.

A poster sponsored by the student government titled "We Will Never Forget You," with class photos of each victim, is plastered throughout the hallways. Every student is given a copy.

Katie is admitted to a psychiatric hospital after her mother discovers slash marks on her wrists.

Katie does not speak to anyone there, communicating in hushed monosyllables and slow head motions, but she begins to regain weight on a diet of Pedialyte.

For ten months, she keeps to herself, looking for patterns in the blue dots on the wallpaper that insulates the institution's patients from the outside world. Group therapy sessions at the hospital are not optional, though Katie remains silent, zoning out among the blue dots as other patients take turns picking at old scabs.

At the end of summer, Katie is on a bus returning to the hospital after a field trip to a park. The bus passes by her old high school, which has re-opened. Class is letting out for the day. A traffic guard wearing a bright orange vest holds up a sign and the bus stops in front of the campus' east entrance.

The bright primary colors of the students' clothes are radiant in the afternoon sun. The roar of adolescent voices rises and ebbs and rises. Liberated by the final bell, the students spread apart and collect together in conversation and physical interaction. A group of girls in sweats tries to stack themselves into a pyramid. A few boys are playing a game of football in casual formation.

The traffic guard lowers his stop sign. The bus's hydraulic brakes release with a loud hiss, and the bus trundles forward, back to the hospital.

That evening is group therapy. At the end of session, the facilitator asks if anyone has any final thoughts to share. Katie stands up. The facilitator smiles encouragement while her eyes shout trepidation.

"Katie is going to share! Everyone, be quiet. We're ready when you are. Don't be afraid, hon."

Katie speaks. Quiet at first, with each word her volume increases until her voice fills the room.

"The Declaration of Independence is an important document in America's history. It represents the beginning of America as a country, and also contains the ideas that became the basis of our government. It was written by Thomas Jefferson and then signed by fifty-six representatives at the Continental Congress in Philadelphia on July 4, 1776. In making the case for independence from the British Empire, the Declaration expresses the values of self-government and individual liberty."

~Matt Braynard

The Woman in The Tree

Feet were planted beneath the ground
calves invisible inside the wood
bark grew shiny where the feminine body
prepared to expose a hint of thigh.

There it was a shapely ass
and the line of her spine rose up and
surrendered again into the tree
shoulders neck head concealed.

Until the arms were freed
yielding to the organic design
hands splintered into a multitude of
fingers budding green into the blue sky.

~Lianne Kamp

Do You See?

Do you see wain in the foxlight?
Do you glimpse the turbulence of the moon?
Do you recognize the vulnerability of sunlight?
Do you descry the essence of contemplation in the dead of night?
Do you behold the majesty of this moment?

Does it see you?
Does it penetrate the darkest corners of deviation?
Does it espy your far-reached cry?
Does it sight the glimmer of an entity's flash?
Does it survey the night only to find the darkest corners of your delight?

Did she notice the vain dash of an incandescent soul?
Did she ponder at the flash of an unseen tail?
Did she wonder at the creak of an unsuspected branch?
Did she start at the call of an unending voice?
Did she associate with the appearance of an incapable vision?

I saw the brevity of the advent.
You saw the flicker of an innocent spirit.
He saw the malice of the shade in the sunlight.
They saw the strength of *vis animi.*
It saw the deviation of your spirit into the darkness of midnight.

~*Caitlyn Mlodzik*

Ghost Town

History's for sale, non-refundable,
you can have it for just a penny.
Don't mind the bullet-riddled signs
or the vandalized windows.
Not part of the Old West,
it has no mystique—
no dead outlaws.
Here, silence
abides.
And with it,
a sense of lives
lived in that stillness.
People dwelled quietly
here, not in desperation,
but in doubt of what the future
might bring. It's not their ghosts, but the town's
own, that lingers to see the mortgage paid.

~Deborah Davitt

Wicked Waltz

Born in the age of phonographs
in a small sinister place that was
in the middle of Inwood, Indiana
where secrets were better left
unspoken because of the pain
with a name like Ambrogio
black flocked velvet vest
a lace cravat and a top hat
shoulder-length acorn hair
parted zig-zag in the middle
black crow resting on shoulder
with a rather scary-looking
chrome skull walking cane
in a room full of waltzers
noticed the ravishing mollisher
the lovely Selene standing alone
near a covey of sunflowers
lavender and charcoal ruffle skirt
blood-red vampire hunter rosary
obsidian eyes full of death
and maroon lips slightly stained
a henna facial tattoo on top
of skin with a bluish tint
intrigued and up for a challenge
leads her to the dancing room
caught up in twirling and circling
spinning round and round
bodies like tops circling the room
he starts to feel a tad dizzy
unaware that she had sprayed
herself with holy water

~Lorraine Cipriano

My Commencement Speech to the Inwood, Indiana, Home-Schooled Class of 2016

Dear Inwood, Indiana, Home-Schooled Class of 2016:

Today you come out into the world as graduates, leaving behind the musty corridors full of old newspapers and windows covered in aluminum foil, the malformed lot of you squinting into the sun like the dreaded molemen of old. Fear not, for soon you will be moving right back into your parents' basements. The woogie has met the boogie, my friends. Although the hellscape of Chicago beckons many of you, most of you will settle into a sedentary life of obesity and ass sores. I'm afraid you will remain under-employed unto death, where the healthcare industry will harvest your organs and the oil industry will boil the rest of you down for use in the internal combustion engines of our clogged interstates.

Still, there may be some hope. "Inwood, We Trust!" goes the cheer, and many take comfort in the town's slogan "Why go to Plymouth When You Could Die Here?" Perhaps, fellas, a nearby junior college will allow you to gain valuable knowledge of woodworking. This will come in useful as you sit on the porch, drunkenly yelling at the giant feral cats silently stalking you from out in the weeds, desperately whittling a spear to fend off their impending pounces. Being outside in the fresh air will do you good, although that is where most of the drownings take place. It is accurate to say that free and perpetual pornography may be the best gift and closest thing to female companionship you ever get.

Ladies, stay away from I-80 and the smiling men driving cargo vans at all costs. Smell the daisies, but keep a .38 tucked in your boot. There are industrious men in Inwood, but most of them are either dentists or in the meth business, a symbiotic relationship to be sure. To paraphrase Margaret Mead, never doubt that a small group of crazy-ass white guys can change the world, indeed, it is the only thing that ever has.

In short, your future lies before you, one that could be idyllic and peaceful here in dear old Inwood. Some say go to college, where you would hunker slack-jawed with your ear buds blasting gibberish, your crusted fingers maniacally texting about the perverse mating habits of your peers. Some say get a job, but all the best ATMs have already been robbed, and your poor grammar and spelling skills from Hom Skool have left your ransom notes a jumbled, illegible mess.

Ah, but what about hope? Well, perhaps you will marry rich. Perhaps I have been too hard on you and your chances out here on the open ground. Now is the time to dress in formal clothes and dance awkwardly, to make promises you will not keep, to play air guitars. Look around, this could work. Here in Inwood there are some trees without blight, some roads without potholes, and some sidewalks without cracks. Our housing stock is pretty good, and our lawns are mostly kept up. It is quiet most nights, and the sporadic gunfire is nearly all innocent plinking. You may have a future here. You could possibly raise a family.

I'll probably see you at the bar, home-schooled class of 2016. All seven of you. Your future stretches out from the minute I buy the first round, and maybe the second and the third. You have choices to make. I have something I'll want to show you out back. Be a good ancestor now.

~Joel Haskard

Pileated

His hand is in the rapid hammering
as if his touch still carpentered my world,
shaping with router and band saw
the wood that grew from the black humus.
His eye is in the black seeing centered
in this flying aimed at fulfilling hunger
from what tunnels or bores into the trees,
just as his sight straightened the cut with
right angles measured by steel square.
His voice is in the near-mad laughter
of being freed into feathers, unknowing
forever in the reincarnation of spring
from migrations beyond these woods,
like the gentleness his wit became when
he had moved three times past death.
I sit on our porch each morning, waiting
his return from the night as a shadow
flying from nothing into the something
of my seeing, hearing. His presence
is fantastic, like the brief half-memory
of last night's dream before the sunlight
chases it into the very darkest green.

~David Anthony Sam

Inwood Today

before that restaurant opened
there was another restaurant
in the same spot
a different name
same type of food
but less expensive

that shop selling shoes
used to sell books
and that convenience store
was once a service station
when the town supported two

There is no tree
that is just a tree
or a house
just a house

if you look
you will find the perfume of past lives
in every reincarnated
building
every lawn

On that bathroom door
Down in Plymouth
Lois came home
to find her husband hanging
and the baby crying
alone in the crib
You may live there now
and never hear that story

Gerald sat drinking some java
in his favorite diner
but when the cops came in for coffee
he panicked and slipped a dime bag worth of joints
between the cushions of the seat
so if the cops stopped him

he'd be clean
and when he came back the next day
the joints were gone
the diner is also gone
and it is now an empty field
with the weeds growing higher

That song
once played as an LP on a turntable
and then on tape
then CD
and now downloaded to a MacBook Air

it has been danced to/sung along with/appreciated over a Chardonnay

Steve and Natalie had it sung at their wedding
and it played in the background
when Bill spent the night with Lorraine
for the last time
before they both moved away
in different directions
their own trail of tears

I don't believe he's spoken to her at all
in the last 20 years

Does each generation
see different possibilities
in the spaces they transverse?
in the structures they colonize?

And is it only old men who remember
when cigarettes cost 40 cents a pack
and everyone smoked.

~Albert Katz

The Flag Bearer

One morning when he woke up
He felt like a triangle
In a rectangular world.

The black milk of the night
Refused to clarify, templates
Fell apart and froze.

Standstill was the motto
That morning. He knew it,
He enjoyed it.

Being different, he thought,
Gave him an edge. He
Was a flag bearer.

~Joseph J. Kozma

Alone in This Place

"They'll kill you, and I'll be here in the woods all alone and abandoned." ~Grimm
(TV Series) NBC; *Season Two, Episode 19, "Endangered."*

I can't relate to the concept of bomb shelters,
hiding underground with a year's supply of food,
ten-gallon jugs of water, antibiotics, a mattress
on the concrete floor.

My biggest fear is surviving.
Alone. In this Place.

When my mother was a child,
a cyclone tore through her Midwest town.
The neighbors shouted out, summoned her
to their cellar to ride out the storm.

When the beast stopped howling,
she crawled out from the cellar,
searched the street for signs of life.

No mommy to hold her hand,
no daddy to lift her up above the rubble.
Only a room —house no longer attached,
and a door —still closed.

She opened this door to her bedroom
to find the sole survivor of the storm —
her doll, still sitting pretty upon a pink
and white checkerboard quilt.

My biggest fear is surviving.
Alone. In this place.

~Shawn Aveningo

Open Your Eyes

I had been feeling sad and lonely. I decided to go back into the past and visit my childhood home.

When I arrived, my sister, mother, and brother were sitting at the kitchen table having a meal. I walked in and said, "Hello."

They welcomed me warmly and asked, "How have you been?" I felt secure and comfortable being welcomed home.

Soon my father made an appearance, asking, "Why are you here?"

"I was feeling sad and lonely. I needed to see my family again."

"You need to open your eyes and see the truth. What you see is not reality." He motioned for me to open the front door.

I opened the door and peered outside. What used to be lush, green grass, plentiful trees below crystal blue skies had been replaced by a vast wasteland. There were no lush grasses, no trees, and the sky was dark with pollution.

When I turned back, my home was no longer recognizable. It had transformed into a run-down, shabby old barn.

"Daddy what does this mean?"

"The keepers!" he answered. "They breed us. They maintain us. They keep us around for food."

His parting words, "Open your eyes!"

~Shirley Smothers

Second Memory

It's dark and big and dauntingly unfamiliar considering I had known it for so many months. A dark, big stairway. Much darker and bigger than it's ever seemed before, though the sun shines freely through the fragmented half-globe window at the top of the door leading to the front yard where the world still breathes. The light coming from the lone window seems only to shine on those three bottom steps. The absence of clothes would frighten anyone, let a-lone [a] four-year-old looking at her father. Despite the darkness and the plush new carpet threatening to hide what lies within, dozens of tiny scattered capsules are astonishingly conspicuous. The darkened stairway grows and grows, the distance to the naked man on the stairs grows and grows, a child's silent scream etched in every false crevice of the old farmhouse walls. There's no movement in the corridor, not even a stolen breath, perhaps only a stolen breath never retrieved, though the silenced scream grows larger with the lengthening stairs, the ever-darkening corridor, sunlight shimmering on these three bottom stairs, bright blue pills scattered around an utter naked rawness that only seconds before had been—or had it only seemed?—warm and familiar. The atmosphere has substance, I can feel it—viscous, heavy—and breathing becomes more like drowning, the air too saturated. Saturated with a lost breath, so many years ago, my absent scream for lack of the requisite breath. It tastes of red-hot metal, bitter and searing through every up down up down up of the stairs and through frozen eyes and the now-empty air. It heats and grows, the corridor and the four-year-old herself, moments from a blistering implosion. An exquisite, erasing implosion after which none of this would exist. An implosion caught in the back of a child's throat and choked on in that breath not taken, never able to reach my world and wash it of all this. Never able to erase. A memory. A formerly familiar stairway, never again warm and comfortable and safe, endlessly growing and darkening with every passing day. An assuasive breath still not taken. A hollow breath, empty, hot—and hot and far too far too far too late—puffed on in its stead. And too late. And far too late.

~Heather Heckman-McKenna

What We Sow

They finished the ring road when I was young,
but I remember its dirt surface scarring
the desert, the barricades.

Later, we drove along it; turned east at
the intersection where ritzy houses
stood atop promontories, sneering down
on those who passed.

Sagebrush gave way to older homes,
shaded by thirsty, non-native trees;
small ranches where horses and cows
watched the cars go by.

Then the semi-urban heart, a mall built
in the sixties, where the parquet floor kicked
up wooden rectangles, loosened by steps.

Since my father's death, no reason to make
my visits anything but virtual;
I drive my childhood on Google maps:
ranches subdivided, horses gone.

The oldest houses remain surrounded
by chain-link fences that rich folk scorn,
and the new homes? Manicured, with thirsty
green grass.

They tore the mall down years ago; left an
empty lot where it stood, a ghost circled
by chain link, and sagebrush grows where asphalt cracks.

No one here cares that they've overbuilt,
that the water supply won't sustain them.
They don't know that they're dying, that they'll reap
what they sowed.

They killed the small town to build a city
on its grave, but never had a plan they
could stick to, so now the city's slowly
dying, too.

And I close the map, happy to have left
the biggest little city, a tumbleweed
that took root elsewhere.

~Deborah Davitt

Lovecraft Baby

Sickly bodies produce the sickest lines
a yahoo from back east, evilly divine
or is that divinely evil, he ain't no gent
he's an agoraphobic shaman from Providence

His pen is his savior and his door to the world, an
unwell magician of the tentacle horde, he rots in a
prison of his own design
a New England master or monster divine.

~Joshua Medsker

We Pass

gas stations, grain silos, a small cemetery,
telephone poles marching single file,

mills, a bowling alley, fast food chains
with names that we all recognize,

a maze carved into a corn field, red barns
protected by Pennsylvania Dutch hex signs,

homes, over-populated parking lots, a pickup truck
flying a miniature flag from its tailgate,

two-tone cows, West Main Street,
imperative slogans telling us which cola to drink,

roadside attractions – a railroad museum
and the oldest turkey farm in the nation,

a placard advertising real estate,
saying *Rental and Sales* on one side

with *NO WAR NO WAR* on the other
in a black scrawl that looks like its dripping.

~*David Russomano*

Inversion

Almost the exact opposite
of those birds you hear
singing in nearby hedges,
but can't see:
      this hawk,
perched on a low-hanging branch
unobscured by leaves,
its talons sunk in grey fur.

When the hooked beak drops —
hydraulic digger breaking ground,
typhoon gutting a beach house —
the squirrel
      resurrects,
tap dancing, electrified,
but the picture is muted,
scene without soundtrack.

~David Russomano

Fat Wet...

Fat wet
snow
flakes fall

softly lost

on ground
unfrozen.

Gray skies,
bare trees
black with water,
smoky breath,
stinging ears,
summer a thought

lost in a shiver.

~Bob Carlton

Johnson Grass...

Johnson grass,
wild lettuce,

white puff
of thistle--

untended, the ditch,
low border
between
upper mowings--

~*Bob Carlton*

Catch

He asks, less subtly, what is the meaning?
It's true money doesn't always fall from the ceiling
but he can't beat the feeling.

(I'm a pretty picture on the wall,
You've made me seem that small).

His eye on the TV, the other on the phone,
I age painfully like an overdue loan,
Or a fed up, washed out crone.

(I'm a pretty picture on the wall,
I find empty space when I fall).

~Linda Sacco

Heart-Shaped Lollies

I arrive
At the Station.
Heart-shaped lollies
Stuck to cement floors
Now appear at the bottom of my shoes.

The sun
Has turned them into a mixture
Of sweet nothingness
That children slip into.

My train arrives.
On board:
Baggage,
Hearts, atom-sized,
Hearts, atomic.

The announcement
Has changed my destiny:
"The baggage is too great
And not capable of holding you."

Tickets are non-refundable
And heart-shaped lollies
Keep me stuck to cement floors,
Waiting an age for what's mine.

~Linda Sacco

The Ecology of Duck Death

It was poor design that killed the duck in the end. A fairly human estimation of how much could get done in a day without bothering to factor in the hours of curiosity.

So when, inevitably, this human fell behind on his chores, all the ducks on the farm had to face their appetite. It didn't take them long to remember their wings and glide over the fence into the neighbor's garden. And there they took to devouring strawberries instead of snails.

It had to be done.

They were run down, caught, and their wings were clipped.

Normally, this wouldn't harm a duck. They'd go about waddling their usual way. Muscovy ducks in particular aren't much for flying. They're from the tropics, they stay still. So when this single duck sought the abundance of a particular cement reservoir, he stayed.

This reservoir has four walls a meter high. It's been leaking from the base for years. Only a few inches of water stand at the bottom. Without wings or long legs there's no way out.

Once inside, the duck felt her beauty. She delighted in looking down on her throne of decayed weeds and posing for everyone who could see her on it. If she could have spoken, her only gripe would have been that no one stopped to visit. Not the clouds running on. The songbirds always held their distance. The waning Moon high in the daylight couldn't wait to dip into the horizon. Although the duck worried about how fast she was eating there was still duckweed in abundance. She would welcome anyone to share the reservoir. Even when a pair of frog eyes poked above the surface, the duck eagerly waddled closer.

But, to survive, the frog can't play. The frog won't get to know you. You are a danger to the frog. Forever and always. He won't acclimate to your presence because you stand still on ferns. The frog is watching. He is forced to find his escape. This particular frog scraped himself along the cement until he met the leak in the reservoir and got away.

Outside the walls, the frog still couldn't relax. He kicked and swam in search of cover. Immediately he found mud for cover. He caught his breath and waited out his nerves. He logged every movement in his new gulch. His nerves wouldn't calm. It was greener there, but it was still dangerous. Cold set in. The frog raced up into some hyacinth roots, looked about, darted towards some grasses, looked about, and poked his eyes up through the lush green.

There, nestled in the watercress, he felt a marginal safety and the calming of the sun. And in his contentment he pooped.

And, you know, poop's gonna break up. Most of it drops in place but a bit of it always flows down with the current. And sometimes, on this land, a small poopchunk diverts from the irrigation into a pond. And that's where it settles down with all the other poops and feeds the anaerobic seal. And the anaerobic seal, since this pond's modeled on a bog- do you know about the anaerobic process that creates bogs?

Assuming you don't, it's a bacterial process in which the organic material growing in a flooded plain dies back and is then eaten up by bacteria without the presence of free oxygen. And this process under constant flooding maintains and protects the anaerobic bacteria which, I'm given to understand, maintains the soil impermeable to water. It's basically, a free method of storing ninety-nine percent of your water without having to use plastic or concrete. And you can feed it with poop.

And what does the pond have to say about this?

The pond says, "Listen up bud. I've been digesting poop now, going on three months. And it's not glamorous. But if I don't do it the humidity drops. And every morning there's dew on the ground thanks to me. You feel that frost? No? That's me. And you see our new friend, Avocado? She couldn't grow in the cold without me."

It must have been true, too. Where the rest of the woods held back their expectation of warmth the avocado felt the sun reflected on the small pond and like all things that feel the sun, she quivered. That little warmth let the avocado stretch out enough to do what she always longed for which was to eat fully from her roots and breath deep from her leaves so she could grow closer to everything that sustains her. This avocado dreamt long ago of the day when she could caress the pond's bank and swore she'd be pretty when it happened. She'd pump every spare cell she had into her berries.

But as life is hard, her berries fell. And it's important to understand that the Avocado is a proud tree. Everyone who knows her personally knows not to mention there's one less treasure in her hair. We scuttle forward, retrieve the avocados in silence, and we thank her. Then we move on.

And when the geese spotted the avocados they rolled on as if they weren't there. To the untrained it might seem that geese are sympathetic to the avocado's feelings. But geese don't care. They ignored the avocados because in that moment they were all about gooseberries. In that moment their purpose in life was to roll strong and pilfer gooseberries. No one stands in the way of the goose.

But a goose's memory isn't their strongpoint. They had watched the gooseberry harvest from the far side of the fence with glib yaps and a few yammers just a few weeks prior. Then, they'd been let in and they'd gleaned what was left. And still, at the sight of bare gooseberry bushes, these geese squawked their mightiest displeasure. In ritual calls, back and forth, rhythmically, they squawked and squawked back. They let loose and bit branches to let them have it. They rolled on back to the avocados where they bit at them too, just to see them broken. They rolled away, those hungry beasts, nipping at torn grasses as they went. Looking for something new to charge. That's about when they spotted their friends the pigs.

They have fine days. Those pigs. There's a, a nodule on some roots. If there's nothing else to eat they can spend whole minutes with their face underground smelling it out. It's a snack, I suppose. They taste a bit like, chickpeas? They look like chickpeas. When the geese rolled up, stretched out their wings to make themselves huge, squawked like mad and charged, the pigs didn't notice. They didn't notice until the geese bit their ears. And the geese held so fierce to the pig's ears that the pigs dragged the geese off like earrings while they whined and scampered. When they got far enough away the geese let go and returned as champions to the gaggle rolling spaciously by.

When finally, the geese had passed, the pigs trotted back and stuck their faces right back underground.

"They're rhizobium." called the human. But the pigs didn't care or answer.

With his head rested on the end of a shovel the human let his mind wander. He'd always been a bit jealous of the pigs. Pigs are so unaware of everything they're not eating. And he always felt such human pressure to see the whole. It never did him good. What he wanted was to live like pigs eating rhizobium. Or potatoes. Or ryegrass. Or really anything they like. Which is most things.

But focusing on the pigs always dragged the human out of the moment. He remembered too clearly that the real and physical pigs were actually hungry and he should already have their next day's paddock ready. But, even if they whined another day and scarfed down less rhizobia than they could eat, and even if he had to feed them more grain than he could afford, it was worth his distraction. This human has always argued that his distraction enriches his life. That day, it didn't teach him much. But, if he'd have worked straight through to nighttime he'd never've chuckled at how big of jerks the geese can be, and he wouldn't have remembered that you can provide a small part of a pig's diet from yet another thing that's already underground.

"Just think about your stomach pigs." the human mocked, "Don't worry about all the legumes you're dismembering. Whine and dig. That's all you lovelies do." And he mimicked their whines with his own high-pitched approximation. "HHmmm HHmmm HHHMMmm."

That they heard. He hadn't spoken pig until then. The pigs ran over to the limit of the electric fence and whined in chorus "hhHHMMMmmm."

'Really?' he thought.

"Bad luck pigs." he told them. "I'm thirsty." And he made his way back to the reservoir. But knowing the adorable faces pigs put on when they're sad, he made the mistake of looking back at them before leaning over to take his drink. They hadn't moved. They were still standing at the limit of the fence. Quiet, sluggish and staring.

"Keep whining." he called and eager to get away from their stares he leaned over to drink. Instead he locked eyes with the duck.

"You still stuck?"

The duck cocked his head. Expression saying, 'Welcome!'

"Don't you wanna come out? .... You think I won't get in there after you 'cause I'd get my feet wet and I don't have your marvelous plume.... Uh huh. I'm on to you. Gimme a sec." said the human, and set off.

There's a closet in the barn filled with food and along beside it is a few fresh logs laid against the wall, hidden beneath that are corridors between the wood where free reign is given to mice who dart from their hollow door to the stores in the closet. And inside the closet, because the silly human thought that it would help to lift the bags up on chairs; the mice relish a good climb. This day the human heard the mice scuttling over the bags of grain and jumped over to the doors. He threw them open and then danced and shouted in the hope that if he danced and shouted long enough the mice would feel too afraid to come back out. But they scuttled into the breaks between the stone walls. There they watched and waited him out. The human grunted, left the doors open, lifted a log on his shoulder, grunted one final warning and set out.

And off the human went with his log, chuckling at how confused the mice must be that he kept adding and then slowly robbing their cover. Wrapped away in his own mind, he knocked the log against every possible obstacle. But that's what's great about a log. You don't have to worry about it. You can bang it against trees as you walk. Drag it along. Drop it in a reservoir to rot with its end set up over the wall as a bridge out of the reservoir. And, mistreat it though you will, what does the log do? It uses its last energy in life to consolidate nutrients and transport them out. Even if they steep out into the water instead of back to the roots. It never minds. It's the duty of the log to support you.

And so did nitrogen leach to the reservoir like tea. She was carried and lost on the current. And nitrogen, one should remember, had lived so long and in so many ways she could almost be called immortal, could no longer tolerate freedom. Yet, it was only in these phases of transition that she came to realize how much she valued the time she spent in a structured system. And more than that, learned how much she missed her brother carbon and longed to be once again beside him in that great system beyond themselves. And as she was primed to bear the fate of the frog and be cast from the reservoir into the next great wild, the next great something appeared. It was a cell inside a duckweed who gave up hydrogen just to have her.

In some ways of looking at it the duckweed ate the nitrogen. I like to think that's what duckweed does. It just goes around eating nitrogen. But duckweed does boring things too. Like eat heavy metals to purify water. Make protein. Cover water like skin to remove mosquito egg niches. And mostly, as comic as it seems to me, duckweed does get gobbled up by ducks.

I think ducks can eat nothing but duckweed and not die.

And this duck did. She ate it up so fast it didn't have time to grow back. So instead of food she saw the reflection of the human spying on her. He hadn't left after he dropped off the log. He sat and watched the duck for hours hoping to harvest his anecdote about what the duck did that time he left the log in the reservoir.

"What're you gonna do when your food runs out, duck?" asked the human.

The duck wasn't worried.

"There's just not enough food in there long term. You've gotta get out duck."

The duck was content.

"You like it in there, don't you duck?" Sucking his teeth, the human waved the duck away. "Enjoy the night." he said. And headed home.

But night is when the courage of the fox flares. And when the fox found the duck he froze on the precipice of the reservoir, weighing his hunger against his fear of swimming. While the duck was briefly excited to have a visitor.

Finally, the log served its poor design. It was a bridge out.

~Diego Reymondez

An Ordinary Morning

The sun, gold like
Liquidized stones, almost
Called lava, found its way
Between the leaves
Of maples just finished
Bleeding sugar freely;
It was a beautiful morning.

Mornings are like that
On days when eternal
Syllables work their way
From the scriptures through
Modern contingencies
Forming a day while killing the night.

Just an ordinary sunrise
without bravado, predictably
Boring in ecstatic magnificence
As you feel like stretching to
The sky to put your blanket
Over the sun.

~Joseph J. Kozma

Dutch

Darren Daulton crouched behind
the plate, ligaments in his knees
crackling like campfires
in a primordial forest.

he'd been pulled from the shadowed alleys
of Philadelphia and pushed
squinting into the Miami sun,
like a broken nose on a mannequin,
like glass on the beach.

warming up he caught without a mask, spitting black
through splintered teeth. at bat

he ground down like an old man
fighting with a rusted lugnut
on a tractor wheel, muscling
the ball
into the right field stands.

whyn't you do that in the game, asked the gawky kid, the
million-dollar kid, the kid
just back from the
All-Star game.

that ain't my job, he said, looking
like a tree stump in a coastal forest.

looking like a man-shaped patch
of forest.

like molded loam and ligneous
clusters and the moving shadows
of living things.

like a man who the woods
had eaten—a frog
in the throat
of the woods.

what *is* your job asked
the kid, looking back to the other kids,
the kids
who knew enough
to look away,
to fiddle with the laces on their mitts.

my job, said he, and the sky went black, my job, he said, and the blackness
bulged, like bulbous eyes…

my job is
now or never.

and the kids, their eyes
like coins, for the first time then
they saw

the thousand dawns
like burrs
in your eyes.

like handfuls
of your hair.

like a thousand
staggering dawns staggering
up off the beach at midnight.

do this now
said Dutch Daulton. do this now
or die. you will die. you will
do this, do this now, and/or
you will die.

and those boys, these
pretty pretty boys grew teeth and took
the field with hearts and eyes

already punctured in their minds.

~*Adam Phillips*

Graveyard Polka

"Listen, now," Victor said to the cab driver, "you drive to the front gate and wait thirty minutes…" Victor paused and looked at the western sky, now fading from a deep orange to purple. "Wait fifteen minutes," he continued, "then come back for me."

"Look, pops," the driver said, "I'm not letting you out of my sight until you pay the fare."

"Fifteen minutes," said Victor. "Then you pick me up, take me home, and I pay you. Not a penny before." He opened the door and carefully slid himself out of the back seat.

"No deal," the driver said. "Besides it seems kind of creepy leaving you in the middle of a cemetery so close to dark." The driver's brow furrowed, drawing his bushy eyebrows together, and he tugged at his wild beard.

"Oh," Victor mocked, "what are you afraid of you big baby? Do you think the ghosties will come and get you?"

"Watch your mouth, old timer," the driver said, "or you'll be walking home."

"Who are you calling old?" Victor said. "Step out and I'll show you who's old." Victor struck the cab with his cane, a glancing blow that did no damage, but he stumbled backward, barely catching himself before tumbling to the ground.

"Hey," the driver yelled, "Watch it."

"And what will the big baby do?" Victor poked the cab again. "You do what I tell you or you won't get paid."

"Fine," said the driver. "Have a nice walk home, old fart." The tires squealed, and the cab was gone before Victor could swing the cane again.

"Who needs you anyway?" Victor said. He unfolded a piece of paper and held it up to read the directions by the fading light. He turned left and began reading off the names.

Harrison, Rose, Perry, Teague. "Aha," said Victor, "There you are Mr. Teague." Victor bent down and ran his hand along the top of the double stone. With his stiff fingers he traced the engraved letters on the left side of the stone. "Hello, Alma," he said. "I hope you won't think me an old fool for what I'm about to do."

Victor stood straight again and looked at the right side of the grave marker. A snowflake fluttered in front of his face. The dusky sky was beginning to sparkle with tiny crystals, but Victor knew his business would not take long. He took off his overcoat and draped it over the final resting place of John Tyler Perry then leaned his cane against the stone.

"Douglas Redmond Teague," Victor said in the voice of a judge passing sentence, "I vowed forty years ago that I would do this." Victor held his arms straight out and began to move his feet, a slow shuffle at first then he began to pick up each foot and cross it over the other. He turned around and clapped his hands, humming a tune with a name he had long forgotten. The snow falling around him, now larger flakes and more of them, gave his dance a misty dreamlike quality.

He took pains not to step on Alma's side of the grave, but as the spirit took him Victor became more animated than he had been in years. He considered a leap in the air then thought better of it, but while executing a half spin, Victor's feet slipped on the now wet grass, and he came down hard against the Teague's headstone.

Victor saw a flash of stars when his head hit the stone, or maybe it was just the sparkling snowflakes that swirled around his head. Was it really this dark already? He tried to sit up, but his stiff body wouldn't cooperate.

"What the hell were you just doing, you old fool?" came a voice from behind him. Victor craned his neck to see the deceased Mr. Teague leaning over the tombstone that bore his name.

"What do you think I was doing, you dumb Irishman?" Victor said, "I was dancing on your grave."

"You call that a dance?" Teague asked. "I've seen better steps on a ladder. Besides, the writing on the tombstone faces away from the grave. I'm buried over here." Teague pointed to the ground on his side of the tombstone.

"It still counts," Victor said. "I vowed forty years ago to dance on your grave for taking my Alma from me, and now I've done it."

"You're crazy, Dabrowski," Teague said. "I didn't take Alma from anyone."

"It was the Knights of Columbus dance in the summer of 1975," Victor said. "We saw Alma across the room and I nodded to you."

"And?" said Teague.

"That nod meant I was interested in her," Victor said. He crossed his arms across his chest for warmth but none came. "I saw her first."

"Listen, Victor," said Teague, "This is the first time I've heard any of this. As I remember, Alma and Ellen were standing together, so when you nodded I thought you wanted us to go meet the two of them."

"Ellen?" said Victor.

"Alma's cousin," said Teague. "They even look alike, though with your eyesight..."

"There's nothing wrong with my eyesight," snapped Victor.

"No," said Teague, "It's just as good as your dancing. Always was."

"My eyes were good enough to see you leave with Alma," Victor said.

"Yes," said Teague, "That you did see." He rubbed his spectral chin and looked into the frosty night sky. "But as I recall you disappeared for more than half an hour and left me alone to meet the ladies. I just happened to hit it off with Alma. When she had to leave I walked her to her car, which is what you saw, but then I went back in and spent the next hour telling Ellen what a great guy you were."

"I went out for a smoke," Victor said, "And to work up my courage I had a second then a third. Then I saw you leaving with Alma, and I never went back inside."

"Dabrowski, you fool," Teague said, "Are you telling me you really didn't see the two of them standing together? And for forty years you've held a grudge and waited to dance on my grave?"

"Yes," said Victor. "But at least I gave up smoking that night."

Teague threw his head back and gave an Irish gale of laughter. "Good for you, Victor," Teague said, "Good for you. Those things will kill you." He patted his tombstone. "See." Teague laughed again. "Oh, but God, don't I wish I had one now." He looked skyward and added, "Not that I'm complaining."

"I am such a fool," Victor said.

"Oh, Victor," said Teague, "You should have come to the house more often when we invited you,"

"I couldn't," said Victor, "I didn't want to stop being angry with you."

"Maybe you would have met Ellen again. She came over when she was in town."

"Oh, Red," Victor said, "You were always a better friend to me than I was to you."

"Nonsense," said Teague.

"It's true," said Victor. "I was always jealous of the way that women seemed to take to you right away. They flocked to you with your bright red hair and your big Irish laugh. I just wanted something that you couldn't have."

"I wish you just had said something forty years ago, Victor," Teague said.

"The wasted life of an old fool," said Victor. Victor's voice was increasingly dream-like and took on the heavier Eastern European accent of his youth.

"Your life hasn't been wasted, Dabrowski," said Teague. "And it's far from over. Look at your successful career and your leadership in the Rotary Club. Who was the force behind the fundraisers for the School for the Blind?"

"Red," Victor said, trying to raise his hand. "Could you give me my coat?" Teague fetched the overcoat and draped it over his friend. "Thank you," said Victor, "I'm tired now."

"Listen, Victor," Teague said with a note of concern in his voice, "I don't think it's such a good idea for you to go to sleep. Try to stand up and walk around a little."

"Maybe I should just lie here," said Victor. "They wouldn't have to take me far to bury me."

"You know, Victor," Teague said, "Ellen is widowed now and lives here in town." Victor opened his eyes and looked at Teague. "I think she would like it if you called her."

"What would she want with an old fool like me?" Victor slurred.

Teague felt in his empty pockets. "They don't bury people with pen or paper," he said to himself, and then he began rifling Victor's pockets. "Don't you go to sleep, old fool." Teague said. "Do you hear me, Victor? Don't you go to sleep, old fool."

"Old fool. Old fool. I knew it was a bad idea to leave you in the cemetery so close to dark." Victor stirred as his body was lifted from the ground. He licked his near frozen lips and tried to speak.

"What are you afraid of you big…" Victor passed out, and the burly cab driver toted the old man's limp body to the cab.

Victor woke warm and comfortable. He lay on a soft pillow and heard a gentle but steady beeping. "Red," he said through his sleep fog. "Red, are you still here?" A warm hand grasped his and Victor opened his eyes. "I was just talking to Red," he told the woman standing at his bedside. She looked at him with a concerned smile.

"The cab driver found you on Red Teague's grave, Mr. Dabrowski," said the woman, who seemed to be near Victor's age but wearing it better. "He brought you here to the hospital."

Victor stared at the woman and his eyes grew wider. "Alma?" he said.

The woman smiled and shook her head. "No, Mr. Dabrowski. I'm Alma's cousin Ellen Maguire."

"Forty years," said Victor. "Forty years. Please call me Victor." Victor looked at her, amazed that she looked so much like Alma. "But tell me, why are you here?"

"The hospital called me," Ellen said. "It seems that they found a note in your coat pocket that had my name and phone number on it."

"Red," Victor said, a smile spreading across his face, "You old dog."

"Excuse me," Ellen said.

"Oh, forgive me," said Victor. "Red gave me your number. I hope you don't mind."

She gave Victor an indulgent smile and said, "Not at all, Victor. Not at all."

~B. C. Nance

Dear Dr. Kevorkian

Dear Dr. Kevorkian:

I've followed your extinguished career for years and was at wit's end with anger when that publicity-seeking DA terminated your career and sent you to prison and not even a prison where you could have aided in executions. Now thank god that's ended, so I'm writing to request your assistance. I'm suffering from a fatal disease with no hope of recovery. Some days are unbearable, and I'm afraid to travel, so can you visit me in Boston to assist me in taking my own life? If you're too busy, which I can understand, will you please recommend the best way to do-in myself?

Thank you.
Very truly yours,
Kermit Remkit, AB. ADD. DID. OCD. PTSD.

Dear Family and Friends,

Bet you're surprised to hear from me and hope this missive is reaching you at an opportune time. Been meaning to write to you for years but you know what happens, stuff gets in the way and before you know it your life is flashing before your eyes and you don't know where the time went, well I know, it followed all forty time zones or what and just burned out. That's life for you. I'm sure you understand.

I sure would like to have seen you one more time, but I'm dying from an incurable disease that has been causing me more pain than joy, and it will only get worse, so I'm writing now to beg your assistance, just a little advice, please, before I'm put in a nursing home, where it will be out of my control, I'm going to end my life but, because I live in a state where assisted suicide is illegal, I'm looking for a way I can do it myself. When I wrote to Dr. Kevorkian, I got the following response:

Dear Mr. Kermit Remkit:

Dr. Jack died in 2011. In any case, he would not have been able to help you as he was forbidden to give advice of this kind as a condition of his parole. Maybe your natural death won't be as bad as you expect. However it ends, we wish you the best of luck.

Margie Mirage
Estate of Jack Kevorkian, M.D.

That was very inconsiderate of him to die prematurely, of course, but what can you do? We all have to go sometime. So can you give me an idea on how to do it? I'll be eternally grateful. I hope you and your family are well.

Love,
Kermit

Dear Kermit,

Oh my God. Oh my God. I can't bear the thought of losing you. Please. Please. As hopeless as you think your condition is, there's always hope. There has to be hope. Have you thought of journeying to Lourdes? Every day, the sick are cured of diseases after doctors have given up on them. Don't give up on yourself. I'll pray for you.

You want to enter heaven, don't you? Not burn in hell for eternity. God doesn't approve of suicide. One of the Ten Commandments says *Thou Shall Not Kill.* That means killing yourself, too. I'm sure you've read the Bible. Here are just two passages that amplify that message:

> *And I give to them eternal life, and they shall never perish, neither shall any man pluck them out of my hand." (John 10:28)*

> *Be not overly wicked, neither be a fool. Why should you die before your time?" (Ecclesiastes 7:17)*

My heart is breaking. Life is too precious to give it up. God will take you when He's ready. However, if you must, (who am I to judge) giving that you live in the city, and I'm not condoning this, you could jump in front of a subway train. I'm praying for you in the name of the Father, the Son, and the Holy Spirit.

Amen,
Lydia

Dear Kermit,

I'm truly sorry that you're nearing the end. I haven't seen you for quite a while and do hope the intervening years have been kind to you. I would hate for you or anyone to suffer unnecessarily but, as your former therapist, following New York law and professional ethics, I cannot recommend any method of suicide. The only thing I can say is nobody can force you to eat. I had a patient who went home from the hospital with a terminal diagnosis and didn't want to go through hopeless treatment and intense pain, so she just stopped eating and drinking and died eleven days later. She hired people to moisten her lips and mouth and clean her when she became too weak to get to the bathroom. You still do that even after you stop eating. She also had her legal affairs in order and left a note that her actions were determined solely by her to take the onus off of caregivers and family. I hope all goes well.

Warmest regards,
Luther Hurtle, MSW. PhD

Dear Kermit,

Oh well. You've lived your life so precariously, I'm surprised you've lived this long. If you want to save money (ha ha!) I recommend the following:

Jump from a high place. A bridge is one possibility, but there is the risk that you may not die. Better to jump from a high building, from at least the thirteenth floor (marked fourteenth in most buildings.) If you want to experience the greatest thrill, jump from the roof or observation deck of a really tall building. People who jumped on 9/11 experienced the advantage of a ten-second freefall. Nobody got to interview them on whether or not their lives flashed before them, but I imagine you could do a fair amount of review in that time.

In case anyone's watching, you may consider doing flips or barrel rolls or summon Superman by wearing a cape and spreading your arms and legs in a headfirst tumble. Remember to smile.

You might want to bring a cell phone and tell someone what you're feeling on the way down. That snippet could go viral, giving you a once-in-a-lifetime chance at ten seconds of fame. Just don't call me — I'm not proficient with electronics and would probably mess up the recording.

Now, many people will think you're a maniac, but some might realize once you're gone that they actually did love you.

'Til death do us part,
Your *second* ex-wife,
Betsy

Dear Kermit,

Your news makes me sad. Too bad you can't visit. When was the last time? It seems like just yesterday. It must be thirty years. Time just flies by. Our lives are so busy. You were married to Betsy.

I live in New Mexico. Suicide is legal here. But you have to live here. I researched this when Cecil escaped. He was my little love. A coyote got him. I wanted to follow. Gaylord talked me out of it. He's my parrot.

Get a can of helium. Like they fill balloons with. A plastic bag. Tape. Valium and anti-gag medicine. Put bag over head. Seal with tape. Inhale helium. It won't take long. Don't change your mind halfway. You'll get brain noodles. And keep do-gooders away. They might stop you.

Good luck. I'll think of you.
Your friend,
Allison

Hey Kermit,

I bin lookin for you. you tink da 50 grand you cos me just spit, huh? youse lucky I dint fine you. if youse a man, you git a 22 and lode it wit a hallo point. Put in you mouth. ame it at you brane. Skwese da triga. you won't feel a ting. if yous a chiken I git youse sombody do it fer 5 grand. Is cheep no? best a luk.

Elbert Treble

Dear Kermit,

Lucy and I were wondering what happened to you when you didn't visit our new place. We're enjoying it like all get out. We sure don't miss the snow and our new pool is the cat's meow. We thought maybe you had the flu or something. Didn't realize it was so serious. We're both sorry to hear about your condition. I didn't show Lucy your question about taking your own life. She woulda birthed a cow, you know what I mean? She can't take things like that with her nervous condition. I gave it some thought, though. Naturally since I was an electrician, hey you should see the Christmas display I rigged up. Best in the neighborhood. People around here want me to set up their lights for next season. I bet I could make enough to buy that trailer Lucy and I always talked about. Then we could see the world – all 48 states. Too old to drive to Alaska.

As to ending it all, you remember that penny shock machine in Nill's Store you used to enjoy so much? It made me think of the solution for you. Fill your bathtub with nice warm water, may as well be comfortable, plug in a lamp with no bulb, turn it on and drop it in. That would beat the thrill of that shock machine, I guarantee you! Good luck. Maybe we'll see you in heaven. But even that place would be hard pressed to beat what we have here. Sorry you couldn't join us before you go.

With all our love,
Peter and Lucy

Dear Kermit,

Get some rope, tie it firmly around a branch a few feet above your head, make a noose, (see attached diagram) stand on a chair, slip your neck into the noose, and kick the chair over. For faster results, climb high in a tree and jump with the noose around your neck to free fall fifteen or twenty feet. This will break your neck resulting in nearly instant death. You've seen this in old Westerns, I'm sure. For additional pleasure, do this while playing a recording of Billie Holiday's "Strange Fruit."

Hanging loose,
Your old friend,
Bart

Dear Mr. Remkit,

It has been such a long time, my old friend. Where have you been keeping yourself? Perhaps it was something I said. If so, I wholeheartedly apologize. Never too late for that, is it? I find it difficult to fathom that you would wish to do such a dastardly deed as to end your life. You wouldn't kid with us, would you? Why would I think that? As a gentleman, one must take you at your word. My advice is to put your head in an old-fashioned oven and turn on the gas as we used to do before we discovered how to sex children in the womb.

Sorry we can't be together again. Farewell, my boy. I wonder what you'll come back as. My guess: a raven.

Your humble servant,
Hash

Dear Dad,

Is this another one of your tricks? You never told me you were ill. If it's true, and you're sure you have to do it, make sure your suicide looks like an accident. I recommend that you crash your car at high speed into something solid like a giant tree, and don't buckle your seatbelt. In your old car I don't think you have airbags to worry about. And make sure you don't kill anybody else. If you don't like that idea, take pills. You may be able to get a doctor to say it was a natural death. But don't leave a suicide note or your life insurance may not pay. Let me know if there's any way I can assist you.

Before you go, please send me a note with the name and contact information of your lawyer, so I can let him know where to send my inheritance.

Hugs n kisses,
Abby

Hey Kermit,

I'm sorry to hear of your problem. If you're sure that you want to end your life do as Nike says, just do it. Couldn't help that. Anyway your question comes at the right time. There are plenty of ways to end your life, but why not go out in style? I just received a shipment of genuine knockoffs of samurai tanto knives. You've heard of hara-kiri, haven't you? The most honorable way to go. I've enclosed a brochure of what I have available. I'd recommend the Golden Emperor model. I'll personally sharpen the carbon steel blade so you get a clean incision.

I also happen to have instructions that I copied from the samurai bushido honor code on the fine art of seppuku (hara-kiri), which I'll throw in at no charge. Sorry there's no video, but you're a smart guy and I'm sure you can figure it out. You want to get it right the first time.

If you have someone who can film you doing it (be sure to dress properly and don't be afraid to smile) I'll pay good money for the exclusive rights to use that video.

Even though we haven't done any business in years, I'm going to miss you. Best of luck.

Sayonara.
The Closeout King,
Rocco

Hi Kermit,

You're still alive? Who woulda thunk it? Why'd you wait until you're dying to contact me? I'm sorry to hear that you're suffering, so I'll try to help you.

You were always interested in nature. As it happens, I became a park ranger and have traveled the world, exploring rain forests and other habitats as well as hosting many scientists in our national parks.

So, maybe it's a crazy idea, but have you considered a natural death by wildlife? I'm not talking about being eaten by a shark, crocodile or polar bear though, with global warming, they need all the help they can get. No, I'm thinking about a small venomous creature that can be brought to you.

My first choice would be the African black mamba, whose bite can kill a human in minutes, but this is a large reptile to try and sneak through Customs and getting an import license would take too long. The new world coral snake might be a good choice. My friend Harry would like to record and monitor your death if you choose this option. as it's an uncommon phenomenon and, just think, you'd be advancing science. He'd be happy to bring you a bunch of them, so your death would be assured.

Harry could also obtain South American poison dart frogs. Amazon tribes use the poison they excrete for their blowgun darts to kill animals. You can die just touching them. I wonder how many people died before figuring that out? Considering your name, wouldn't death by frog be perfect?

So think about it and if any of these strike your fancy let me know. In any case, I'll be sorry to see you go.

Your childhood friend,
Forest Foster

Dear Kermit,

It's about time! I wish you had done this before we met. It would have saved me and everyone else you were with a lifetime of agony. In your case, do what those monks did during the Vietnam War: soak yourself with gasoline and light a match.

Good riddance!
Faye

Dear Family and Friends,

Mr. Kermit Remkit is no longer with us. As per his wishes there will be no memorial service. He asks that in lieu of flowers, you please send a contribution to the Kermit Fund, supporting assisted suicide. You can pay through PayPal with this link, https://www.paypal.com/x.kermit or you can mail a check to the Kermit Fund, PO Box K9, Boston, MA 02100.

He thanked you in advance and wished each of you a long, healthy life.

Sincerely,
Kerry Kidnot, Esq.
Executioner of Estates

P.S. If you contribute $499, the fund has authorized me to send you a true collector's item: a miniature engraved silver urn containing 3 1/2 grams of Kermit's ashes. Supplies limited.

~Gustaf Berger

Bones of Blue, Eyes of Gold

if I were to redefine myself
redesign everything from the inside out
i would start with bones of blue
not soft, gentle, pastels
but deep, intense, midnight blues
that hold the mysteries of the stars
the history of the universe
a place to hide my darkest thoughts
my deepest desires
bones to resonate like blues saxophones
vibrating their lowest tones right down
through the floor

someone else might want to make
muscles of coral, thousand shades of red,
but I want malachite, variegated greens
strength and beauty combined, sculpted

platinum is my preference for a heart
no corrosion, no soft parts to fail
or break at some hint of love lost
an enduring precious core, mi corazon

and so with other systems, the world's richest hues
a neon yellow brain, electrical circuits flashing
plumbing and pipes of fluorescent orange
circulating titanium white around and around and around
ending with eyes of purest gold
so I could see through deception
recognize goodness in everyone I meet

if I were my own designer

~j.lewis

Mysterious Ways

I got called to speak for the Lord in the summer of '92. Boy, what a summer that was, let me tell you. I hadn't said a prayer in I couldn't remember when, and I was a sinner in the worst ways—different women, sometimes by the day, sometimes for money, and plenty of liquor and all the lines we could find. When you're not a servant of the Lord, raising heck can be a good time, let me tell you.

But it wasn't my ways that caused the Lord to call my name. I had a buddy, a good buddy, who helped corral the women and suck down the liquor and snort the lines, sometimes right off their you-knows. Like I said, boy, what a summer. For a day job, me and my buddy installed telephones for big companies, before telephones turned smart and quit needing as many wires. There's something to be said for a phone you can't put in your pocket. Suits left their work at work back then. Now they hardly have time for my sermons, punching away in the pews.

My buddy, he had the sweetest kids—a boy and a girl—and the darndest doggone ex. But she'd popped out two good kids. The boy was bug-eyed and had to wear glasses a fourth-inch thick so his eyes wouldn't drift towards his nose. The girl, I'm not ashamed to say, was as attractive as her mother, had her mother's smoky blue eyes. But her hair was chopped all to pieces cause her momma refused to pay for a proper cut.

"She don't want her daughter to out-shine her," my buddy told me. "That's how batty she is, jealous of a five-year-old."

Gerald was his name, my buddy, Gerald with the big you-know and the handsome nose was how the girls talked about him. They just said I was Gerald's friend, the one with the OK face. Now Gerald, he wasn't so much nuts as just not ready for the responsibility. He'd had them kids before he was twenty-two and split from his ex—Crazy Susan he called her, instead of Lazy—by the time they were twenty-five. If I didn't know all I knew, I'd have gone after her. The woman had the sexiest head of thick, curly hair—on top and below from what Gerald told me. And boy she could shake her hips when she walked down the grocery store aisle, in blue jeans and high-heeled pumps, batting her eyes like the crazy ones sometimes do.

When they got the divorce, Gerald didn't even fight, satisfied with getting the kids on weekends, not wanting to feel guilty about the women and the liquor and the lines and all. I couldn't blame him then and don't judge him now. A man who don't get that out of his system is doomed to fail anyhow. Sad thing was, Gerald didn't get the time to, but for some reason, the Lord let me have mine. Like I've learned, He works in mysterious ways.

That's how I came to get called to preach, the day Crazy Susan was doing cartwheels in her front yard. Not that it had to do with me directly, but I was with Gerald putting in phones when our boss drove out to deliver the message. Gerald's old next-door neighbor had called headquarters, saying she'd never seen Susan quite like this.

"Sir, she's doing flips in the grass," our boss said the neighbor lady told him. "And if that don't beat all, she's naked from the waist up."

Gerald asked me to come along, and I didn't mind getting away from the cords and the suits for an afternoon, although leaving the AC in the middle of July in Alabama ain't never a good idea. But heck, I'm not gonna lie—I wanted to see what Susan looked like from the waist up.

"She's been telling me she found the Lord," Gerald said, chain smoking Pall Malls and weaving his pickup in and out of the cars through town. "But she's probably just off her pills. Doctor know'd it from the time she was three."

He shook another Pall Mall up out of the pack.

"You regret her or the kids more?" I asked.

"Both the same, I guess." He thumbed his handsome nose.

"Think if you'd met her later, it would've gone different?"

"Some of us just ain't cut out for it, for no time," he said and flicked ash into the breeze.

When we turned onto Gerald's old street, I couldn't take my eyes off Susan's handfuls bouncing with each cartwheel. She had on tight jeans that sucked the rest of her in and spilled her top half out in a flattering way. Gerald slammed his hand on the wheel a couple of times before we pulled in. He flung his cigarette and slung open the door. I stayed put, seeing as how it wasn't my business, other than he was my good buddy and had asked me to come along. But dadjimit it was hot, even with the windows rolled down. I was sweating like a prostitute kneeled down for communion and couldn't hardly find a dry spot on my white button-up to wipe my forehead.

I did my best not to keep on staring at Susan's you-knows—the house was nice too, a one-story vinyl with a sturdy cement porch and wrought iron posts with Christmas lights wrapped around 'em. All the blinds were shut, but I could see the boy's bug eyes and the girl's gapped bangs peeking through. Susan was smiling wide, showing her long white teeth, while her feet flew over her head, her you-knows still the finest I've seen.

"Can't you get by without all this Goddamn attention?" Gerald hollered. The whole neighborhood could hear him plain as day. "How embarrassed you think them kids are gonna be, when they get old enough to know better? You're the worst damn thing ever happened to me."

Susan stopped, put her hands on her hips, and pouted her lips into a frown. Her you-knows were shining with sweat, and Gerald's white button-up was soaked through. Then, without as much as a sound, she marched over and punched Gerald smack in the gut. He doubled over, and to beat all, she bent down and rubbed her handfuls in his handsome nose.

"You miss these don't ya," she yelled louder than she had to, so the neighborhood could hear too. "But what do you care, huh? You get to ride the merry-go-round all day, don't ya? With whoever the hell you want. What about me? You don't think I want to get out and play?"

Gerald pushed her off him, not hard, just enough to get her you-knows out of his face. He clenched his fists like he was gonna sock her, and I wouldn't have blamed him, even now in my preacher's suit. But he went in for the kids instead. He came out the screen door with the boy and the girl, one under each arm, both of them bare foot, with only their clothes on their backs and the boy's bug-eyed glasses.

Susan did a few cartwheels to the porch and hopped up the steps. She slammed the screen door. I reached across to open the driver's side so Gerald could push the boy and the girl across the bench seat, their legs splayed around the stick shift. I told him to get on in the pickup, but he had other ideas.

"I'm gonna set her straight," he said. "This is the last time she does me this way."

I'm not making light, but he turned out to be right. Susan had the pistol raised with two hands before he even got to the porch. I couldn't help but notice how her you-knows looked that much bigger, squeezed together that way. I yelled for Gerald to get down, but that wouldn't have done any good—he was as naked to the bullets as Susan's you-knows. I've not seen another man's head blown off since, and Lord willing I won't have to, all that red and insides. To this day I can't even stomach a forkful of spaghetti or meatloaf at the church potlucks.

The kids started hollering and carrying on something awful, but their momma was as quiet as she could be. She'd come off the porch and was standing in the grass over her ex. I grabbed the boy and the girl up in my arms and hustled them to the neighbor lady who had her head poked around her screen door, yelling at the top of her lungs. I told her to hush up and call 911, even though Gerald was deader than a doornail.

Jogging back, I saw Susan kneel down in the grass and turn her eyes up to Heaven. I stood over her, but she looked right through me. I'd always called her blue eyes smoky until I got a good look at 'em up close, for what they really were—shattered, like they'd been smashed into a million shards of blue.

"The Lord is my shepherd," she mumbled to the sky.

"Susan, get up," I said. "No more faking."

That word—*faking*—must've clicked cause she pushed herself up, the knees of her jeans grass-stained. She glanced over at Gerald, who was face down, shot with his own gun, the only dadgum thing he'd left her, come to find out. The sight of him didn't seem to shake her.

"All sins are equal in the eyes of the Lord," she said.

"What in the hell kind of nonsense is that?" I was getting pretty worked up with my friend laying there dead, but mindful of that pistol still in her left hand.

Susan locked eyes with me, reciting Matthew as steady and sure as if she were at the pulpit: "I say to you that everyone who looks at a woman with lustful intent has already committed adultery with her in his heart."

"Shitfire, woman. Don't mean you put a bullet in his head."

"Don't be afraid," she said. "He is always with you, even now, until the end of time."

The sirens were blaring but she still wasn't fazed. I searched Susan's shattered eyes, wondering if the Lord really was speaking to her. Even now, having been called, I can't tell you for certain if He was or He wasn't. To tell you the truth, I wouldn't be surprised if He was, seeing as how Gerald was living the way he was and Susan being better off separated from the rest of us. But I can tell you for certain that I heard the Lord in the yard that day, telling me to follow Him.

Like I said, mysterious ways.

~LaRue Cook

The Flash Flood

It came at night. I was in bed, counting sheep like Pa taught me. The next day was a school day. I could hear Ma and Pa in the living room, watching the news. Then, there was a rumbling, faint at first I thought it was simply thunder approaching from a distance. But it grew louder and louder and I never realized until too late—for it happened fast, so fast—that that was the sound of water rolling from the sea towards the city. The last I heard of Ma was her shouting my name and footsteps hurrying up the stairs. I never saw her or Pa anymore after that.

The water exploded through the door that opened from my room and into the terrace. The wooden panel flew out of its hinges with a giant crack. The wave lifted me up from my bed, slammed me into the wall, and pushed both me and the wall backwards, the slabs giving way to the force of the oncoming rush. The room quickly filled to the brim, I was choking under, flailing my arms in an attempt to swim, but I was tossed by the strong current. I felt I was going to drown when I started gulping salty water in between gasps. But it was surprisingly quiet under the water. Almost peaceful, I closed my eyes.

And so it happened, when I had stopped fighting and gave myself up to the surging flood, I was lodged between the branches of an uprooted tree. The current carried the tree, with me caught under its foliage. I hanged on. I was comforted, hugging a branch, hidden inside the leaves. The tree rode atop the swell.

It didn't take long. The flash flood passed like a giant wave. But when it left, I did not recognize our city anymore. Blocks where houses used to stand were left empty, the cellars gaping mouths on the ground. A few buildings, those made of concrete, withstood the beating but their glass windows were all broken and the things inside in disarray. Mud covered everything. People were everywhere: dead, unconscious, those wounded and couldn't stand, and those who, like me, were only bruised but walked dazedly amidst what were left. Until others came and rescued us.

They made those of us who were left homeless live in a high school situated in a neighboring town, converted as a temporary shelter for the victims. Uncle Tomas, Ma's brother, found me and he took me to live with his wife and son. They lost Cathy, my cousin, older to me by four years. For two days I went around and scoured all the classrooms, noisy with children running around and their parents either watching them with disinterest or conversing with each other, hoping to find my parents. But Ma and Pa weren't in any of them. Finally, Uncle Ben took me to the municipal plaza, hoping to find Ma and Pa among the rows of dead bodies laid on the grass and pavement.

We didn't find my parents. I just told myself, maybe Ma and Pa were carried by the flood when it flowed back to sea and buried them deep underneath the seabed. Uncle Tomas didn't find Cathy. Most of the people who were walking through the bodies did not find their own families, either. Then again, it was hard to be certain which were your relatives. A lot of them had lost limbs, legs, even faces.

After three days, the unclaimed were buried in one grave, there in the same plaza, where a monument now stands in their memory.

This is all I remember about the flood.

~Raymund P. Reyes

Made in the USA
Charleston, SC
11 August 2016